INHERITANCE

Clinging to God's Promises in the Midst of Tragedy

COREY RUSSELL

FORERUNNER PUBLISHING

KANSAS CITY, MISSOURI

Inheritance — Clinging to God's Promises in the Midst of Tragedy
by Corey Russell

Published by Forerunner Publishing
International House of Prayer
3535 E. Red Bridge Road
Kansas City, Missouri 64137
ihopkc.org/books

Forerunner Publishing is the book-publishing division of the International House of Prayer of Kansas City, an evangelical missions organization that exists to partner in the Great Commission by advancing 24/7 prayer and proclaiming the beauty of Jesus and His glorious return.

ISBN: 978-1-938060-40-3
eBook ISBN: 978-1-938060-41-0

All emphasis in Scripture quotations is the author's.

Cover design by George Estrada
Interior design by Dale Jimmo
Printed in the United States of America
28 27 26 25 24 23 22 21 20 19 18 1 2 3 4 5 6 7 8 9

To Josiah "Nash" Russell

Your brief life and sudden death have changed us forever. We will never fully be the same again, yet we have great hope and expectation for our lives here on earth and our reunion with you in eternity. We love you and miss you so much, little man. May Jesus be glorified through our story. We also pray that God would raise up one hundred million "Nasharites" all over the earth who would believe and see the greatest outpouring of the Holy Spirit that the earth has ever witnessed.

* * *

We want to acknowledge all of the people who have been a part of our journey from day one. Your words, prayers, gifts, acts, and love have carried us for these last five years. Thank you.

Contents

Invitation

Allen Hood

IT WAS A NORMAL COREY RUSSELL SERVICE where he took a famous prayer-movement psalm and exploded all of our charismatic niceties. I can still hear him thundering that Psalm 42 is an invitation into immense suffering, where, in the depth of our pain, God forms the groan of true intercession. Suddenly, the picture of a sweet fawn drinking from the still brook of God's peaceful pools gave way to the biblical reality of seasons of panting and gasping, where deep calls unto deep in the roar of God's shattering waves, where the cry for deliverance is a matter of life or death.

The ways of the Lord are very personal. The Word always seeks to become flesh, and the messenger, if he or she lives long enough, will become the message. Psalm 42 became more than a sermon; it moved to real invitation. The phone call would come only a few months after I heard his initial message on the psalm. Dana, Corey's wife, was heaving, "He's dead, Allen. He's dead. I cannot find Corey. He's dead. Corey's in London and I cannot find him, and Nash is dead." God's breakers were just beginning with the death of their nine-month-old son. The roar of His waterfalls would continue for years, not months, as the crushing would go deeper and then deeper and then deeper still.

I had a front row seat to how the Lord used a previous messenger from the hills of Bethlehem to lead my dear friend through the darkest nights of loss and despair. David's words became the inner language of Corey's heart. The tears and words produced in Corey as he clung to, prayed over, and preached on these five psalms were nothing but extraordinary. The Lord will not forget these deep callings. They are precious to Him. They are precious to me. I hope you will glean from Corey's journey as much as I have. It is God's most precious work in him yet.

> Deep calls unto deep at the noise of Your waterfalls;
> All Your waves and billows have gone over me.
> The Lord will command His lovingkindness in the daytime,
> And in the night His song shall be with me —
> A prayer to the God of my life.
> Psalm 42:7–8

Allen Hood is the executive pastor of Forerunner Christian Fellowship and the associate director of the International House of Prayer Missions Base of Kansas City.

Foreword

Bob Sorge

LIKE COREY, I UNDERSTAND LOSS. In my case it wasn't the loss of a child, but still it's been deep, bitter loss. And like Corey, I identify implicitly with Psalm 119:92, "Unless Your law had been my delight, I would then have perished in my affliction." That's not just a nice verse for me, but it's something I've experienced.

Processing loss biblically has been the great challenge of my life. I'm persuaded that losses submitted to Christ become in His hands the material that turns events into a fabulous plot. It's the hope of a divine story that is carrying both Corey's family and mine — and, I believe, many of you.

Corey and Dana Russell are spiritual giants in the faith for whom I have the utmost respect. They walk in holiness and integrity, and they practice the presence of God. And yet, they haven't been exempt from tragedy. In this book, you're going to watch an exemplary family wrestle with agonizing grief and search to unlock God's purposes in suffering. Because when you're the Lord's inheritance, everything in life is bathed in divine purpose.

Corey's going to take you on a tour of five psalms, and one of them is my all-time favorite: Psalm 18. Every single day I call on the Lord to grant my household the answered-prayer reality of Psalm 18. That psalm vibrates and rumbles with holy purpose.

Psalm 18 is a cut/paste excerpt from Second Samuel 22. However, in the latter case, there's one phrase that doesn't appear in Psalm 18. And it's a phrase that pulsates purpose. Whereas Psalm 18:50 reads, "Great deliverance He gives to His king," Second Samuel 22:51 puts it this way, "He is the tower of salvation to His king."

"Tower of salvation." What a glorious name of Christ!

Jesus has a way of taking earth-swallowing losses and raising them up into towers of salvation. By the time the story's done, it towers as a witness to every generation of God's extravagant salvation.

Not too long ago, I had the delight of touring Taipei 101, which is a world-class skyscraper in Taiwan. The immensity of its proportions helped me visualize what it means when God erects a tower of salvation. I want to mention a few dynamics about skyscrapers that I think can also apply to God's salvation. As you peruse these, may the Lord strengthen your hope in His resolve to build a tower of salvation out of your losses. Here we go.

- Towers are almost always built in city centers and can be seen for miles. Similarly, the witness of your story will one day be seen far and wide by many people.
- With the exception of New York City's Twin Towers, almost every tower in the world is unique. And they're few in number, which is why they stand out in contrast to their

surroundings. The story God is raising up from your life is strikingly one of a kind.

- It takes a long time to build a tower. The taller the tower, the deeper the foundation and the longer it will take to build it. That's one reason saints with the greatest testimonies often have to wait while Jesus sets the thing up.
- Towers are very expensive to build, and they sit on real estate whose market value has skyrocketed. In other words, your story is worth waiting for.
- The tallest towers of the earth attract tourists. They come from all over to gawk, observe, and admire. They're awed by its towering accomplishment. Perhaps this is the spirit behind Psalm 48:12–14, "Walk about Zion, and go all around her. Count her towers; mark well her bulwarks; consider her palaces; that you may tell it to the generation following. For this is God, our God forever and ever; He will be our guide even to death." Zion above is a city with many towers — saints whose lives are a towering witness to God's faithfulness. When the skyscrapers of Zion are all brought together, people will come from all over to count the towers and say, "This is who our God is!"

The greatest tower of Zion, rising high above all others, is the sacrifice of the Lamb. The tower God built with Christ's cross stands far above any other witness, extolling the majestic splendor of God's salvation.

I don't think Zion's skyline is finished. I believe God is still building towers of salvation with the lives of His beloved children. I believe He is building a tower of salvation with Corey and

Dana's story, and I'm persuaded He wants to erect a towering witness to His salvation with *your* life as well. As you walk with Corey through his five-year personal journey, may that confidence grip your heart. God's building something!

Bob Sorge suffered a debilitating vocal injury over twenty years ago. He speaks and writes on God's purposes in fiery trials. Among his many books are Secrets of the Secret Place; The Fire of Delayed Answers; The Chastening of the Lord; *and* Exploring Worship.

Introduction

FIVE YEARS AGO, OUR LIVES EXPERIENCED AN EARTHQUAKE with the sudden death of our son. My wife and I, and our three daughters, are still in the process of walking out of the trauma and pain caused by that moment. God has used five specific psalms to carry my heart, as well as our family, through this season. I believe these specific psalms will prove to be a great strength and anchor for those who are about to walk through a dark night, those who are walking through it now, and those who are trying their best to interpret one they've walked through.

Each one of these psalms carry a specific theme that has massively strengthened me and helped me interpret the passing of my son through the Word of God. God, most likely, has used other chapters and verses in the Word to strengthen you on your journey, but, without a doubt, these are the ones that have helped me the most, and I believe they will help many other as well.

1. Psalm 132: The Promise
2. Psalm 1–2: Inheritance
3. Psalm 91: Protection
4. Psalm 18: Deliverance
5. Psalm 23: Shepherd

This is by far the most vulnerable story I've ever told. It's not over, yet I feel that God wants me to share our story now because many people need it now; they can't wait twenty years. I must tell it while we are still limping through and out of it, to help save, strengthen, and encourage as many people as possible.

I'll be the first to tell you that we haven't done this perfectly in any way. There has been much pain that each one of us has lived in, as well as caused each other, over these last five years. And yet, each one of us has continued to get up every morning, look to Him and to each other, ask for forgiveness, and cling to God and His word that He truly "causes all things to work together for good to those who love God, to those who are called according to His purpose" (Rom. 8:28 NASB).

I'm also convinced that we need more testimonies to come forth from people who are limping their way through trials and tribulations, because of the courage that it instills in those who are going through it themselves. There is a verse in Psalm 119 that I cannot get out of my mind regarding the power of our testimony.

> Those who fear You will be glad when they see me, because I have hoped in Your word. (Ps. 119:74)

This hoping in His Word isn't the puffed chest of those

valiantly walking through a tragedy, but is the continual realigning of a weak heart with God in the darkest of nights. My prayer is that you will be strengthened in your journey by reading our journey and that God's Word would be your anchor above everything else, because if He can carry us, He can carry you.

1
He Is the Author

THIS BOOK IS A STORY THAT GOD HAS BEEN WRITING in and through my life and the life of my family over the last five years. I've written four others, but this is different than all of them. It's one thing to write books; it's a whole different thing when you *are* the book that God is writing, and you are the story that He is telling. It's vulnerable and at times humiliating when you don't get to control the narrative because Someone else is writing the story.

God is truly the Author of our story, and there are certain chapters that I honestly don't like, nor ever want to walk through again. I'm glad that when I got saved God didn't lay out to me my seventy-year Christian journey. It most likely would have overwhelmed me, even caused me to shrink back versus run into Him at full speed. Instead, He spent fifteen years ruining me for the ordinary with His presence, His beauty, His heart, and His purpose before taking me and my family through a very dark night, when I would need the previous fifteen years of history in God to navigate and survive the next five.

In Psalm 27, David declared that a lifetime of making God his "one thing" was the reason he had confidence when trouble hit his life. When he was surrounded on every side by the wicked who sought his life, David wrote that his heart would not fear and that he would be confident in one thing:

> One thing I have desired of the LORD, that will I seek: that I may dwell in the house of the LORD all the days of my life, to behold the beauty of the LORD, and to inquire in His temple. **For in the time of trouble** He shall hide me in His pavilion; in the secret place of the tabernacle He shall hide me; He shall set me high upon a rock. And now my head shall be lifted up above my enemies. (Ps. 27:4–6)

Times of trouble come to every one of us in different forms and in different ways. These seasons come in the form of loss, disappointment, false accusation, betrayal, rejection, temptation, and many other sorts of affliction. These troubles expose every fault line in our lives, and it's here we find ourselves naked, vulnerable, exposed, and desperate to do everything we can to find shelter and security.

These past five years have been the hardest in my life, and I don't believe I'm alone in this. I'm running into people all over the earth who have gone through more junk in recent years than they have in their whole Christian journey.

What is God doing?

Is this coincidence, or is God strategically working through our personal trials in a fallen world to bring out something more, something greater, even essential, for His church? I believe He is. But how do our personal trials and tribulations fit into the big picture? From what I'm seeing God do with me and my family, and what I'm seeing Him do with my friends, I believe that God is raising up shepherds according to His heart who will come forth in the coming days of great revival and great crisis to feed people not just on concepts about God, but a revelation of God that has been "fleshed out" in their lives, marriages, and families.

The last days are spoken of as being days of great trial, great offense, betrayal, coldness, hatred, and deception, yet in the midst of it all God will release revival and glory into all the earth, touching the most broken and hopeless people. Who will carry this glory into the earth? I believe it will be shepherds who have been personally shepherded and forged through their own Psalm 23 "valleys of the shadow of death." They will emerge with compassion and authority to bring heaven down into the most impossible of situations.

In the midst of my darkest night, the face of Jesus as Shepherd has emerged as the predominant revelation, and as He has shepherded me, I've intuitively known that He was raising me up so that I could shepherd this next generation. These shepherds aren't just pastors in our local churches, but will characterize the spirit of all last-days ministry in every sphere, from one-on-one disciple making to stadium-sized gatherings.

Daniel 11:32 states that "the people who know their God shall be strong, and carry out great exploits." When I used to read this, I would picture a group of Navy SEAL Christians who are so strong that no one can oppose them, but the older I've gotten, I've begun to see this group as ones who, in the midst of their darkest nights, encountered Jesus. They broke through a "cheap" knowledge of God into something real that makes weak people strong and anoints them to bring the kingdom to the earth.

I've intentionally sought the knowledge of God for twenty

years. There are aspects of this knowledge that involve new thoughts about God and new views of God, but there is a knowledge that goes past our thoughts and is worked in us through a deep, painful journey that goes a lot slower than we would choose and takes a lot longer than we would choose.

The full revelation of God was not realized until "the Word became flesh, and dwelt among us" (John 1:14). The Eternal Word of the Father had to come and get into the dirty of our experience, our misery, our struggle to lift us out of it. In the same way, God in this hour is bringing shepherds into a place of identification with the plight of humanity for the purpose of bringing them through.

As I will touch on in Chapter 9, the identity of Jesus as Shepherd comes forth in John 10 in the context of the thief who comes to steal, kill, and destroy. I believe God is emphasizing Jesus as Shepherd and is raising up shepherds because the enemy is stealing, killing, and destroying so many lives, marriages, and families in the church as well as the broader culture.

If there is ever a time for Christian marriages and families to come forth, not with a set of "to dos" for how to have the perfect family, but with a testimony of how God carried them through their darkest night, it is now. We desperately need a new level of vulnerability, honesty, and compassion because there are so many weary, harassed, beaten down, and destroyed families currently in the church, as well as in our neighborhoods, who are aching for the tender, restorative touch of Jesus.

> **When He saw** the multitudes, **He was moved** with compassion for them, because they were weary and scattered, like sheep having no shepherd. (Matt. 9:36)

I believe that Jesus is sending shepherds who see with His eyes, are moved with His heart of compassion, and are commissioned to shepherd the weary, harassed, and scattered. These ones will have been formed through their own crucibles of fire. The knowledge of God that changes the way you see, the way you feel, and the authority you walk in isn't gained cheaply or quickly, but is worked out in you through the fire of trial that causes the gold to come forth and the dross to melt away.

2
The Call

I REMEMBER IT LIKE IT WAS YESTERDAY. It was March 16, 2013. I was ministering in London, England, and it was one of the most powerful weekends that I had experienced in a long time. The presence of the Lord was so glorious; I was undone by the activity of God in our midst. The messages I was preachng on the knowledge of God and the prayer movement in the earth were matched by great revelation and conviction among the congregation. I had never been at that church before and felt an instantaneous connection with these beautiful people. I knew that God was up to something big.

The weekend carried a shifting-of-the-seasons feel. The previous nine months had been such a time of prophetic fulfillment with the birth of our son, Nash, yet from the time he arrived, there seemed to be constant warfare surrounding his life and our family. This weekend in London seemed to have a different feel to it, and I was really optimistic that things were finally settling.

On the second evening, right before the service, I called my wife back home to see how she and the kids were doing. The love of my life and best friend, Dana, and I had been married for fifteen years, and we had been blessed with four beautiful children. Trinity was thirteen, Mya was ten, Hadassah was three, and Josiah Nash was nine months.

We'd had Trinity and Mya in our earlier days and then walked through two miscarriages before having Hadassah in 2010. For many years, we had received word after word about a son we would have who would be a son of promise. One of the most important words for us in the season of waiting was given on the seventh birthday of our middle daughter, Mya. It was March 4, 2010, and at the time, there had been a seven-year gap in between our children. Julie Meyer, a long-time worship leader at IHOPKC, brought me into a side room and shared a dream that she'd had on three different occasions; she knew it was time to share it with me. In the dream, I was standing before her weeping, and she looked at me and said, "What you've sown in tears, you will reap in joy." In the dream, she then looked down to my left hand, which had Isaiah 9:6 written on it, and said to me, "Isaiah 9:6 — you know what it means."

When Julie shared this dream with me, I said, "Isn't that 'Wonderful, Counselor, Mighty God'?" She looked at me and smiled and said, "Read the first part." I went back to my seat in the prayer room, opened up my Bible, and the first line jumped off the pages: "For unto us a Child is born, unto us a Son is given." I immediately began to cry as God confirmed deeply to my heart that we would have a son. Words like this built such anticipation for the day we would see it come to pass. On June 26, 2012, that day came.

After many hours of intense labor, our son, Josiah Nash Russell, was born, and I was the happiest I had ever been. An amazing wife, three beautiful daughters, and a son of promise — I was undone by God's faithfulness. We called him Nash after an intercessor named Daniel Nash who was a prayer partner of the famous evangelist Charles Finney during the Second Great Awakening in the 1800s.

The morning before I left for London our whole family had been hanging out and getting our last minute snuggles, and as Dana bent to pick up nine-month-old Nash, her back went out. She was immediately in pain and unable to get up. I'd had to quickly gather some babysitters for the day so that Dana could rest, and then I'd prepared to leave. I remember the last thing I did before leaving was to go over to Nash, who was sitting in his high chair eating his breakfast, and give him a big kiss on his head, telling him, "I love you, buddy." I remember looking back and watching him eat before I left; the moment seemed to last forever. I wanted to keep this memory close to me as I traveled over the next five days. Though the trip wasn't that long, I was in love with this boy. I'd felt the same with all my girls, but I was coming to an age in life of being able to take in their young years more consciously, knowing how fast they go and that in a second he would be running around and not need me like he had at first. Those first nine months with my son were such a time of bonding, as I would share the midnight duties with my wife of feeding and being up with him, enjoying those quiet moments in the night. He was my partner. I had fallen in love.

On that second evening of the trip, I called Dana from London and found out that after having lain in bed the day before, she had felt better and decided to take the kids down to Arkansas to see her parents and let them enjoy the hundred-acre farm. Spring break was going on, and she thought it would be fun for the kids to get on the four-wheeler and enjoy the warmer weather.

I remember our conversation. I remember sensing happiness in Dana that I hadn't in a while. Nash was a colicky kid, so the winter had been long, and Dana was tired. Things were beginning to settle down as Nash's colic was subsiding, and Dana was beginning to feel like herself again. She spoke with more hope as she talked about how beautiful the weather was, how much fun she was having with the kids, and some of her dreams for the next season.

After talking for around thirty minutes, I told her that I had to go into the meeting because worship was starting, and she said that she was going to wake up our little man from his nap. I remember going into that meeting with a sense of peace and hope that I hadn't felt in a while. We had been in survival mode recently, and it seemed that the season was changing. I was truly happy and overwhelmed with God's goodness and faithfulness.

I remember what I preached that night — Isaiah 56 and God making us joyful in His house of prayer, calling all the nations into joyful prayer before the Lord's return. It was one of the most enjoyable and powerful times I've ever had in preaching. There were about twenty nations represented in the room. His presence was so strong, the people were so hungry, and it seemed that every word was dropping like a bomb in their spirits. It was amazing. The ministry time was crazy as the Holy Spirit marked His people in a powerful way. I was undone by all that God was doing.

Toward the end of the ministry time, while I was still swirling in the move of the Holy Spirit, someone came up to me with a phone in their hand and told me that Elcio Lodos was on the phone. Elcio led a house of prayer in London, so I thought that maybe he was hearing what was happening in the meeting and wanted me to pray over him. As I took the phone, Elcio said in a shaky voice, "Corey, you need to call your wife. Something has happened to your son." As soon as I heard this, I began to think that maybe Nash had gotten the fever that came through the week before and had affected Hadassah. I just thought that the same virus had him down, and Dana would ask me to pray for him as they take him to the doctor.

I quickly called my wife. As soon as she picked up the phone, she immediately began to scream, "He's dead, Corey. Our son is dead!" She kept saying this over and over and over again, screaming and crying. I couldn't register what I was hearing. I had no grid, no comprehension. "No, No, No!" was all I could say. I tried to talk, but it was impossible. I tried to ask questions, but she couldn't answer. All we could do was cry together. I told her that I was going to get on the first flight out in the morning and would get to Arkansas as soon as possible.

Words cannot describe what I felt at that moment. Everything ground down to slow motion and each thought seemed to hang for minutes. Numbness began to settle in on my emotions, as I tried to consider that I would never see my son again. I honestly couldn't even register what I was hearing and thinking. It was so unnatural of a thought. I kept thinking kids bury parents; parents do not bury kids.

In the middle of those first minutes, I remember saying to God, "**God, you know what it feels like to lose a son. I need your help**." I don't know where this came from or how. The reality that it was March 16th — 3/16 on the calendar — was highlighted to me, and I thought often that night on John 3:16 and the Father's pain in giving up His only son. This was honestly my only comfort in the mourning — the Father has felt this.

The next hours were a blur of sitting in shock, receiving calls from friends and family. Dana had been reaching out through every social media outlet trying to get me to call, but was unable to. She'd had to bear this for three hours before getting hold of me. We finally found a flight that would get me out of London at six a.m., so I decided to go back to the hotel and see if I could grab an hour or two of sleep before leaving, but that was impossible on this night. I spent most of the next two hours Skyping Dana and the girls. We just sat there, looked at each other, and cried. That's literally all we could do. A dear friend spent the night with them and was my arms and my prayers until I got there.

You cannot imagine the feeling of not being able to be there with your family to comfort them in a moment like this and also be able to pray over them. There is no more powerless feeling in the world than being unable to hold, to cry, and to pray with my girls. It ripped my heart out. Another part of me wanted to lie on my son and prophesy life back into him. But all I could do was cry through a computer screen and keep saying, "I'm so sorry. I'm so sorry."

Several hours later, I boarded the plane from London to Atlanta, and I knew that my life would never be the same. Everything was changing, though I had no idea what that meant. I was met in Atlanta by my best friend, Allen Hood, and I remember sitting in the Sky Club there just looking at Allen, speechless. I remember flying to Arkansas. I remember landing and coming down the escalator, seeing my dad, my brother, and a family friend waiting at the bottom. I just buried my head in my dad and cried. We then made "the drive" to the house. It almost felt like I was outside of my body, watching this happening. It was so surreal.

We finally arrived; I ran into the house and found my wife and daughters. We all grabbed each other and wept and wept and wept, holding one another and crying for what seemed like hours.

We were told that they were classifying Nash's death as a SIDS (sudden infant death syndrome) case, as they stated that they did not know what happened. He was nine-and-a-half months old and was out of the normal SIDS window. A week before Nash passed, Hadassah was taken to the emergency room with a horrible virus. A couple of days later, Nash was beginning to show some signs of slower breathing, but he began to feel better and his breathing returned to normal. I spoke with our family doctor shortly after he passed, and he believed that the virus got into his bloodstream and into his heart.

God, in His kindness, sent us dear friends from Tulsa who had lost two children. One had died in a drowning accident, and the other was hit by a drunk driver. The only people who can really speak into a situation like this are ones who have been through it. This dear family was a gift from God to us and was able to help with clarity, strength, and comfort for our whole family. Their words, prayers, and counsel helped us immensely in those first days. They really ministered to Dana and broke off all the "what ifs." This was massively important for her as we moved forward.

For me, the only thing that brought comfort was talking to Nash and telling him how much I love him. He felt so close to me. I remember taking big breaths over and over again and just saying, "I love you buddy. I miss you buddy. I love you buddy." During those moments over the next three days, time stood still.

The second day I was in Arkansas, Mike Bickle, the director of the International House of Prayer of Kansas City (IHOPKC), along with some other dear friends from the prayer room there, drove the four hours down to see us, pray with us, and just talk. It was such an encouragement and strength, knowing our spiritual family was with us. IHOPKC blew us away over the next months covering meals, helping, and loving in so many ways.

The two more days we spent at my in-laws' place before heading back to Kansas City seemed to fly by. I was literally out of it and couldn't even register all that was happening. I can't think of anything more foreign to the human experience than a death like this. I'm so grateful for all the friends and family who carried us during those first days, handling all of the nightmare details that no parent should ever have to consider.

Nash passed on Saturday, March 16th, and we stayed at Dana's parents' place until the following Wednesday. We were going back to a house with so many memories, so many experiences connected to Nash, that we honestly did not know how we were going to be able to handle it. Once we arrived, I walked through the door into our house and began to immediately sing a song by Misty Edwards titled "Hold Me." I honestly had not sung this song in forever. It came right out of my spirit when I walked into our house, as the Holy Spirit was preparing my heart for the hardest journey of my life. Our family just fell on the floor, held each other, and cried.

We so needed to hear from God as we entered back into life at home and began our journey, and God met us. On the first night back home, my wife had a powerful dream that I believe was the banner invitation over this season and that has become such a source of strength. In the dream, she looked up to the clouds and they began to turn into people. She then saw a man inviting her to come and lie in the grass, look up to the clouds, and see all the people. In the next scene, she saw a hospital with a black tube going up into the clouds. She asked him if she could go see it and he told her *yes*. She went and looked up the black tube and saw a man like a janitor cleaning out the tube — it was getting prepared for her.

As she woke up, she immediately thought of Hebrews 11 and the "cloud of witnesses" that have gone before her. She felt an invitation from the Lord to take her place among the cloud of witnesses who through faith endure. As each witness had a verse in that passage that defined his or her life of faith, she knew that her endurance of this loss would be the "verse" over her life and that God was preparing the way for her. This dream has proven to be a banner over our family, keeping us in hope through this whole journey.

The same first night home, while checking messages on Facebook, she found one that a lady had sent her with a song from Natalie Grant about the loss of a child, titled, "Held." As Dana listened to this song, she was deeply touched and believed that God wanted her to sing it at the memorial service a few days later. Dana hadn't sung in years and knew that God wanted her to sing for Nash. We found out a few days later that during the moments of Nash's passing, a friend of ours was overcome with tears and grieving as she was shopping. She ran out to her car in the rain, got into her van, and began to weep, not knowing why she was crying. When she began to hear this song on the radio, she concluded that this was intercession for the loss of someone's child, not knowing what was happening with Nash at the very moment. Dana's dream and this song proved to be massive encouragements to us in our first week.

I knew that my only "sanity" in the midst of this would be the prayer room. At the time of Nash's passing, I had spent thirteen years giving myself to thirty hours a week in the prayer room, and it was as if I needed all of the history of those years to keep me anchored for the next ones. In Psalm 27, David declares that the one thing he had desired of the Lord was to dwell in His house, behold His beauty, and inquire in His temple, "for in the time of trouble He shall hide me in His pavilion" (v. 5). Our call to making God our one thing and seeking to be in His house is unto us having divine perspective in the times of trouble in our lives. Those times become the seasons where we are lifted high upon a rock and God puts a song in our mouths in the midst of the storm, prophesying the next season into existence.

That first morning back, I dragged myself to the prayer room at six a.m., knowing I needed His presence, His Word, and His comfort. I remember walking into the prayer meeting as Jaye Thomas, the worship leader, began to sing, "I'm holding on to your divine love. I'm holding on, and I'm not letting go. It's not my zeal." This gave language to describe where I was, and I knew that His ability to hold us was the only way we would make it through. I honestly don't know where I would be today without that prayer room and the reality of having the words of God saturating my mind and heart as singers sang and intercessors prayed. Over these last five years, as the singers have sung and the musicians have played, I have cried so many healing tears and been washed with His presence, strengthened, and elevated into the place where I knew it was all going to work out.

I believe that one of the main reasons God is raising up prayer rooms all over the earth is to heal traumatized people through the power of prophetic song. God is raising up prophetic singers in this hour to come forth with song to heal, restore, and deliver people. In Zephaniah, we see the Lord rejoice over His people with singing. The Bible says, "He will quiet you with His love" (Zeph. 3:17). What a verse! Oh, for the traffic in the soul of a traumatized generation to be healed as they sit in prayer rooms across the earth and the Lord sings over them, quieting them with His love!

On the Friday before Nash's memorial service on Sunday, Dana's parents arrived from Arkansas; they were as wrecked as we were. This whole thing happened at their house, and they were honestly ready to just burn their house down because of the pain connected to it. I love my mother-in-law and father-in-law. They have been such a support during all of our years of marriage. As they arrived completely devastated, we had some friends of ours join them with us for a time of ministry and prayer. Sometime in the middle of the prayer and ministry time to Dana's parents, our friends began to highlight the fact that Nash was now in heaven. They then began to lay out the gospel, stating that only through Jesus Christ can we enter into heaven. When asked if they wanted to pray and ensure that they will spend eternity in heaven, as well as be with Nash forever, Dana's parents eagerly said *yes* and prayed the most beautiful prayer repenting of their sins and putting their faith in Jesus Christ. We cried together and laughed together as the Holy Spirit invaded the room. Since this moment, they have been deeply changed, and God has done amazing things in their lives.

Two days later, the "day" had come — the memorial service for Nash. It was March 21st, and as a freak snowstorm came through town, all of our friends and family began to descend on our home. The whole day was surreal; I literally felt outside of my body as the hours went by. The service came and went so quickly. I was blown away by the courage and strength of my girls. My two older daughters both wrote letters to Nash and read them publicly at the service. Dana sang for the first time in years for Nash; she shared about his life and what he meant to us. I was so in love with my girls and their devotion to Jesus — they did amazing. I was undone. We played a video with pictures of Nash set to Rita Springer's "Worth It All." As soon as this started, deep pain and grief mixed with the hope of seeing my boy again. These feelings co-mingled the entire day, and I never recovered.

The next day our friends and family left, and the journey officially began. It's been almost five years now since Nash went home to be with Jesus; to say that things have dramatically changed is a huge understatement. This event shook our family to the core, exposing every fault line in our lives individually, in our marriage, and in our children. We are still here by God's grace, but we know that we will never fully be the same again. These kinds of moments change things forever, and we will in one way or another carry this experience with us for the rest of our lives here on earth. Though we are on a healing journey and many amazing things have happened along the way, we deeply miss our son and long for our reunion in heaven. We will carry the limp of the loss of our son for the rest of our lives.

From the start, I want to state emphatically that I do not believe God killed my son or took my son. However, I believe there is a real Devil who seeks to steal, kill, and destroy us, and he struck at our family in the death of our son. I also believe my son was sick and that, very likely, a virus was in his bloodstream and heart that caused him to die. I look at this event, as well as all tragic events, through the lens of a sovereign God, a real Devil, the choices of men, and living in a fallen world. I refuse to get caught up in the endless vortex of questions that never bring me to an answer, but only leave me angry with God. I've settled it that some questions will not be answered in this life, but will made clear in the light of eternity. From the beginning I've known that I really only have two options here: die or live. I choose to live.

From the moment I received "the call," I knew I had to connect to the bigger storyline of what this meant. I honestly never asked the question, "Why?" though I believe it's biblical to ask. Jesus asked that question on the cross, and there is nothing wrong with it. However, for me, it wasn't "why?" — it was more of "what?" and "how?" as in, "What does this mean?" "What is the storyline here?" and "How do I respond?" Christianity is a war and, in my perspective, we took a hit, so I settled that the only way to take ground was to not quit and to begin to lean even more into God. If the Devil wants to strike at my family, I will make him pay for it by pressing in to see my son's name and story awaken a whole generation.

It was this thinking that was immediately on me following his death. The fact that Nash died on 3/16 gave me great hope in the early days, as I couldn't help but think of John 3:16, that says God gave His only begotten Son so that whoever would believe in Him would not perish but would have everlasting life. To me, 3/16 meant great losses that bring great blessing to many people. I began to plead and ask God for a mighty harvest out of this death and that the kingdom of darkness would be destroyed in a small way through my life and through my son's story.

The thing about a tragedy like this is that when you have five people in the same house who experience the same thing, they will have five different responses. The difficulty over the last years has been to keep everyone together. Some people fight; others will go into flight. Some cling more strongly. Others want to let go. There is no wrong way to process grief; there is just a call to not quit. There are Ephesians 6 seasons when it's not about taking ground — it's about standing, which means not quitting.

The months of March through August came and went with a lot of pain, loneliness, isolation, and anger. I was in completely uncharted territory and felt utterly ill-equipped to lead a family through such a horrible tragedy while at the same time deeply grieving the loss of my son. For the first time in my life, I was unable to fix the situation; that in and of itself was my biggest struggle. I wasn't able to staunch my wife and daughters' bleeding hearts, and this drove me crazy as a man, a husband, and a father. It was this that drove me to my knees and caused me to throw myself on God; I didn't know what to do.

On my first trip five months after Nash's death, I went to Australia for five days and returned around midnight to find one of our daughters in a serious fight with Dana. Desperate for God's wisdom, I woke up the next morning around five-thirty, went to the prayer room, and prayed in tongues for two hours before I heard anything. After two hours, I simply heard the phrase, "Love covers a multitude of sins" (1 Pet. 4:8 ESV). This phrase went off like a bomb in my heart and the reality of covering love served as a word from God about how I was to walk out the next season. I knew of a love that confronts and that fights for, but the love that covers became a deep revelation to me, and I knew it was God giving me my marching orders.

It was this verse, which really opened up First Peter in a wonderful way to me in July 2013, that greatly strengthened and encouraged me to stay the course of suffering, knowing what it will produce. The overwhelming message of First Peter is to "humble yourselves under the mighty hand of God, that He may exalt you in due time" (1 Pet. 5:6). This helped my heart massively, because I could cast all my care on the One who cared for me, trusting that through it all, He had a plan.

In mid-August, while seeing a counselor, Dana brought up the fact that I had gotten a vasectomy toward the end of her pregnancy with Nash. (Dana was on bed rest for the final six weeks of her pregnancy with him, and after fifteen years of having kids, I felt that it was time to stop.) As they talked about this, the counselor felt led to share his story of how he had gotten a vasectomy reversal in Arkansas and how they'd had another child and it was a great blessing. Dana came home and brought up to me the possibility, but I was aggressively against it. We'd had our kids, and I was satisfied with it.

I was leaving later that day to go on a ministry trip to Mankato, Minnesota, with Allen Hood. I mentioned our conversation to him, and we spoke about it but not seriously. After the first morning's session, on the way to meet the pastors for lunch, Allen told me that he thought I should seriously consider it. Just as we arrived and walked into the restaurant, the pastor's wife was holding up her iPhone to show a picture of their family. I noticed in the picture that they had two natural children, then an adopted child, and then a younger natural child. I noted the big gap between the older ones and the younger one, so the pastor's wife told the story of how they'd had the first two and then some miscarriages, which led to the pastor getting a vasectomy. In that time they adopted. After many years went by, the Lord ended up convicting him about it and connected him to a urologist in Arkansas who did reversals as a ministry at a reduced price, as his desire was to see children come forth.

Before I go any further, how many times have you talked about vasectomy reversals at lunch? I doubt many. As she shared their story, Allen started kicking me, and I got flushed in the face — I was starting to face the fact that God was calling me to get a reversal. On top of it all, they'd had it done in the city where I went to college in Arkansas! After that trip, I called the doctor — he'd just had a cancelation and could get me in for the procedure in four days. So within one week, I went from saying, "No way, God," to "God, You want this?" to getting it done. This was one of the clearest things God spoke to us in that whole season. Honestly, when sadness, hopelessness, and despair descend on your life, you hold on tightly to those moments when you see God doing something. We still haven't conceived, but are believing that we will. I believe that there are some of you reading this who have gone through your own dark nights and have received promises, but they haven't been fulfilled yet. I just want to say, "Hold on," because God will make good on His promise.

Around the same time as this, Dana's good friend Stacey Campbell, an anointed speaker, invited her to come to Phoenix to be at a Women on the Frontlines event, to participate and lead some worship. On the last day as they were driving to the airport, a number of these women of God began to prophesy over Dana, breaking off every spirit of death and calling the prophetic voice and prophetic song to come forth out of her.

A couple of days after this conference, Dana received three

songs from the Lord, releasing Nash. These songs came out of nowhere, and we knew that we should record them — God was moving, and we needed to get them out as soon as we could. These songs brought a lot of healing to Dana as well as our family, and we've heard many testimonies of how God used them in the lives of those who have lost children or loved ones. We entitled the album "3:16" to honor the day of his passing.

This little prophetic swirl in late August of 2013 proved to be a huge encouragement to us. Though we would have many dark days ahead, this was a drink in the middle of the desert. We've found over the last five years that God has thrown in these little hope fillers, or "kisses," along the journey to keep us going, and, just when we don't think we can make it another day, He encourages us Himself or through other people.

I will emphatically state the only reason that my family and I are here today is Jesus Christ and His faithfulness, and, specifically, His Word, which has kept us through these five years. He has strengthened us time and again in various ways, but as the months have played out into years, the Scripture has been our anchor, our fortress, our comfort, and our healing. Beginning in August of 2013, God began to highlight and walk me through specific psalms that changed me, piece by piece, and have carried me to the present moment. The next several chapters walk through those psalms. I can't keep them to myself. I want to see the Word of God become the anchor for a generation as they walk through life's storms, as it has been for me. I wholeheartedly agree with David when he said, "**If Your law had not been my delight, I would have perished in my affliction**" (Psalm 119:92 ESV).

Psalm 42

As the deer pants for the water brooks,
So pants my soul for You, O God.
My soul thirsts for God, for the living God.
When shall I come and appear before God?
My tears have been my food day and night,
While they continually say to me,
"Where is your God?"

When I remember these things,
I pour out my soul within me.
For I used to go with the multitude;
I went with them to the house of God,
With the voice of joy and praise,
With a multitude that kept a pilgrim feast.

Why are you cast down, O my soul?
And why are you disquieted within me?
Hope in God, for I shall yet praise Him
For the help of His countenance.

O my God, my soul is cast down within me;
Therefore I will remember You
from the land of the Jordan,
And from the heights of Hermon,
From the Hill Mizar.
Deep calls unto deep at the noise of Your waterfalls;
All Your waves and billows have gone over me.
The LORD will command His lovingkindness in the daytime,
And in the night His song shall be with me—
A prayer to the God of my life.

I will say to God my Rock,
"Why have You forgotten me?
Why do I go mourning because of the
oppression of the enemy?"
As with a breaking of my bones,
My enemies reproach me,
While they say to me all day long,
"Where is your God?"

Why are you cast down, O my soul?
And why are you disquieted within me?
Hope in God;
For I shall yet praise Him,
The help of my countenance and my God.

3

Psalm 42: The Psalm Before the Other Psalms

FIVE PSALMS CARRIED ME THROUGH the last few years, but one preceded them, Psalm 42. Several months before Nash passed away, I became consumed with Psalm 42 and the reality of spiritual hunger. So many of us have made hunger a nice, polite ask for more from God, but it's not. It's a raw, painful, desperate cry of the soul for more of God. We by nature gravitate to the easier, comfortable way, and God has to disrupt us in certain seasons to awaken a fresh cry for more in us. God has always used a scene from one of my favorite movie series of all time, *Rocky*, to highlight this truth to me.

In *Rocky III*, Rocky Balboa is coming off his historic upset against Apollo Creed, and the movie begins with Rocky defending his title belt by beating a bunch of guys who are no competition at all. They are bums, and Rocky is rolling through them. Rocky settles into complacency, thinking he is on top of world and that there is nothing left for him to fight for. He plans to retire. What he doesn't know is that there is an up-and-coming fighter named Clubber Lang who is hungry and desperate to beat everyone so that he can get a chance at the belt. Rocky's manager, Mickey, has seen him and is terrified of the look in this fighter's eyes.

At Rocky's retirement party, Clubber Lang shows up and begins to talk a lot of trash against Rocky, calling him a loser and boasting that Rocky would never beat him. Chaos erupts when Rocky tells him to name the time and place. In private, though, when Rocky begs his manager to let him fight this guy, Mickey turns around and yells, "You can't win, Rock! . . . This guy is a wreckin' machine, and he's hungry! . . . You ain't been hungry since you won that belt!" Mickey walks over to Rocky and tells him, "The worst thing happened to you that could happen to any fighter: you got civilized."

This scene has continually provoked me over my life as a believer. I told the Lord early on to never let me get "civilized" in Christianity but to keep me hungry, raw, desperate, and leaning on Him. I've found over the last twenty years that there will be seasons when God begins to cause a deep hunger to awaken within me, and, for a time, I become disillusioned with myself and others around me as a cry rises, "God, there must be more!" I've come to know that when God wants to draw me into a new season, He will first create a new hunger in me. These preparatory seasons are accompanied by increased amounts of prayer, fasting, and consecration and a deeper groan within my spirit for more.

God answers this cry by bringing me into a new season of intimacy with Him in the Word, zeal for holiness, and a fresh anointing in ministry. I will ride the wave of this new season for three to five years and enjoy many amazing things, until God once more "tenderly wounds my soul in its deepest center," as St. Jo Cross exclaimed in *The Living Flame of Love*, and the whole process starts over.

Sometimes, as we see in Song of Solomon 5, when His voice breaks into our life and invites us to go through a new door, it brings us into a place of suffering that we had no clue was coming nor were prepared for. But in the end, this unexpected suffering releases greater impact, as people who watched come asking, "What is your beloved more than another beloved, that you walk through the darkest of nights unoffended and love Him more in the end?"

In February 2013 I began to feel stirred by Psalm 42, and I knew that this was God's way of preparing for a new season and that a new door was opening. I was excited, on fire, and anticipating a lot of great things would be coming.

> As the deer pants for the water brooks, so pants my soul for You, O God. My soul thirsts for God, for the living God. (v. 1)

Have you ever touched one of those seasons when a deep pain begins to well up within you, panting after God, thirsting after God, and you will do anything for more of Him in your life? When you are grateful for all that He has done in your life, but you begin to realize that you haven't touched anything yet? Hunger is a painful thing as it begins to touch your life. Hunger makes you disillusioned with everything around you, everything within you. When hunger touches you, you can hardly stand to hear another sermon or hear others (or yourself, for that matter) talk anymore. It's those times when you are raw, and the only thing you can see is the gap between His fullness and your emptiness. Hunger for God is, in my opinion, the greatest gift someone can receive. It's when God delivers you from your own evaluation, as well as everyone else's.

This is what David was touching in Psalm 42. He appears to be watching a deer pant desperately for water, and he began to compare that thirsty deer to the state of his own spiritual life. Later on, in verse 7, while watching a waterfall plunging deeply into the water below, David began to compare that to what God was currently doing in his life: "Deep calls unto deep at the noise of Your waterfalls; all Your waves and billows have gone over me."

I love the visuals that David gives us in Psalm 42 — **a panting deer and unrelenting waterfall.** These two vivid pictures give insight into what happens when a person becomes consumed with a vision for more of God in the midst of life's crashing storms. He takes us all on the same journey. He awakens a yearning that will not be denied, and we cry out for the "living God" (v. 2). When you want more than a form, when you want encounter with the "living God," things start changing. Most people like a god they can control, who won't break out with unexpected things, but "living God" implies His prerogative to do what He wants, when He wants, how He wants, and that changes the game on so many levels.

In the many years I've been following the Lord, I've found this process to hold true: God awakens a deep cry inside of me and gifts me with hunger; out of that hunger, I cry out for Him; and He meets me with fresh breakthrough in every area of my life. From 2001–2005, after moving to the International House of Prayer, we were constantly in the place of desperation and hunger, crying out for more of God. Those were years of deep longing, and God met my hunger with breakthrough in many areas of my life, including personal revelation, marriage unity and purpose, family purpose, finances, and ministry sphere and influence. I rode this wave from

2006–2012 in a profound way. In that season, I wrote four books, released three CDs, and was experiencing a level of blessing that I had never in my life experienced up to that time.

It was at the beginning of 2013 that God begin to pierce me afresh with a new hunger for Him. I became disillusioned with my existing intimacy with God, my existing power in God, and began to cry out for more of Him in my life. In that season, because of favor and open doors, I was preaching and traveling more than I ever had; but I was also finding that my capacity and intimacy in the Word and prayer was waning. I did not feel the same unction in my messages. This was so painful. I cried out to God for a new gut-level passion to emerge from my spirit, from God.

The waterfall was about to be unleashed upon my life, awakening a deeper cry inside of me than I knew existed. Watching a waterfall and its unrelenting pounding caused David to say that deep calls out to deep at the noise. It seems to me, as David watched this waterfall crashing down on the water and rocks below, he saw that there was an unrelenting pounding going on in his life orchestrated by God. The "deep . . . to deep" was the depths that waterfall would reach once it hit the water below, and then the same depths reaching back up to the surface. David was saying that God's activity in his life was creating a depth of desperation in him that was simultaneously reaching a depth in God to see deliverance and breakthrough. I would encourage you to close your eyes and picture a waterfall, as well as the sound it makes, as it continually pounds on the body of water below. It's unrelenting.

I specifically remember being in Pato Branco, Brazil, with Allen Hood in February 2013 as God was beginning to awaken this cry in me. Allen prophesied the reality of Hannah's prayer coming upon my life. This has been a deeply personal verse for many years, so I immediately knew that it was about a prayer of desperation for something to be born.

I was expecting a new season of favor, anointing, and authority to come on my life. Instead, I got the shock of my life. Little did I know how deeply we were about to be cut, nor, which we sometimes questioned, if we were going to make it through. Psalm 42 had prepared me for something entirely different than I expected or wanted.

Psalm 132

LORD, remember David
And all his afflictions;
How he swore to the LORD,
And vowed to the Mighty One of Jacob:
"Surely I will not go into the chamber of my house,
Or go up to the comfort of my bed;
I will not give sleep to my eyes
Or slumber to my eyelids,
Until I find a place for the LORD,
A dwelling place for the Mighty One of Jacob."

Behold, we heard of it in Ephrathah;
We found it in the fields of the woods.
Let us go into His tabernacle;
Let us worship at His footstool.
Arise, O LORD, to Your resting place,
You and the ark of Your strength.
Let Your priests be clothed with righteousness,
And let Your saints shout for joy.

For Your servant David's sake,
Do not turn away the face of Your Anointed.

The LORD has sworn in truth to David;
He will not turn from it:
"I will set upon your throne the fruit of your body.
If your sons will keep My covenant
And My testimony which I shall teach them,
Their sons also shall sit upon your throne forevermore."

For the LORD has chosen Zion;
He has desired it for His dwelling place:
"This is My resting place forever;
Here I will dwell, for I have desired it.
I will abundantly bless her provision;
I will satisfy her poor with bread.
I will also clothe her priests with salvation,
And her saints shall shout aloud for joy.
There I will make the horn of David grow;
I will prepare a lamp for My Anointed.
His enemies I will clothe with shame,
But upon Himself His crown shall flourish."

4
Psalm 132: Promise

The preparation season God gave me through Psalm 42 ended abruptly on March 16, 2013, with the death of Nash. Sometimes God begins to awaken a hunger in you, but as soon as you open the door to it, a season of suffering ensues. This is what happened to me. Though there were a few moments of clarity and comfort from the Word of God, it wasn't until five months later, in August 2013, that I slipped into Psalm 132; it consumed the rest of the year. The reality of David's vow and the afflictions that followed were deeply touching me as I began to process my life, my family, my son's passing, and my destiny through the lens of eternity.

When things like this happen in your life, you are wounded to the core of your being, and only the stuff of eternity matters. The reality of my son's legacy, his life, his name, and his purpose became my main motivation in those early days. I so wanted to move heaven with this pain, this prayer, and did not want to miss the opportunity of a season like this, when I was so raw. I felt as if Nash's death cut me and called me back to some of my deepest vows and desires for prayer. It was in this time that I began to reconnect with Psalm 132 in a very deep way.

Psalm 132 had meant a lot to me since my early days of getting gripped with a vision for the house of prayer, but I was beginning to see it as a vow that shifted history and wanted to pattern my life after it. I believe that Solomon, David's son, wrote Psalm 132. In Second Chronicles 6:41, at the dedication of the temple, Solomon prays a portion of Psalm 132: "Now therefore, arise O LORD God, to Your resting place, You and the ark of Your strength. Let Your priests, O LORD God, be clothed with salvation, and let Your saints rejoice in goodness." As soon as Solomon prayed this, fire fell from heaven and consumed the sacrifice, and the glory of the Lord filled the temple.

What was David's vow to the Lord? It was that he would not rest until he found a place for the Lord in his generation. Instead of getting lost in thoughts of Old Testament tabernacles and temples, I want you to connect with David's ultimate desire for God's presence to be manifested in the earth. This is what drove David. This is what God is reigniting in our day all over the earth, and I believe in the same way fire fell on that first generation, so a global outpouring of the fire of God will come upon the church in these last days. This is what burned in David, and this is what I burn for. I long for this desire to consume a whole generation.

As I began to study, meditate, and pray Psalm 132, God's covenant with David in Second Samuel 7 became very dear to me. There are a few hinge chapters in the Bible that carry eternal significance. Second Samuel 7 is one of those. In it, we see King David finally coming to a place of rest after many years of flight, war, setback, loss, and difficulty. He had assumed the throne in Jerusalem and was now king over all of Israel. The whole nation was joined together and, as it pertains to the promise of God, he had "arrived." And yet, David wasn't satisfied with being at rest himself when God wasn't fully resting. This is one of those things that made David different than everyone else. He wasn't just satisfied with his rest in God, but longed for God's rest in his generation. He told Nathan that it wasn't okay that God didn't have a permanent dwelling place in Jerusalem, but was living in a tent. In response, Nathan told him to do whatever was in his heart.

That night Nathan dreamed, and God gave him a word for David. When I read this word, I saw it in a way that I've never seen it before, and was undone.

> "Go and tell My servant David, 'Thus says the LORD: "**Would you build a house for Me to dwell in**? For I have not dwelt in a house since the time that I brought the children of Israel up from Egypt, even to this day, but have moved about in a tent and in a tabernacle."'" (2 Sam. 7:5–6)

When that first question came out of God to Nathan about David, it struck my heart that God wasn't asking in a dry or stoic way if David would do this, but that God was actually moved that this desire would be in David's heart. Instead of "Would you . . .?" I heard, "You would . . .?"

In essence, God was saying, *You mean you would do this for Me? Where did you get this desire, David? I've never asked anyone to build Me a house, and yet you want to do this for Me?*

It's my personal conviction that this desire of David's so moved God that something erupted in His heart, and He gave to David one of the greatest gifts God could give to a man: His Son would become David's son!

> "Also, the LORD tells you that He will make **you** a house. When your days are fulfilled and you rest with your fathers, I will set up your seed after you, who will come from your body, and I will establish his kingdom. He shall build a house for My name, and I will establish the throne of his kingdom forever." (2 Sam. 7:11–13)

God's answer to David's desire to build Him a house was a prophecy that He would build David's house and that David's name and throne would live forever, and that, in fact, the Messiah would come through his lineage and would sit on his throne and would build the ultimate house he was longing for.

God turned the tables on David and said, *You want to build Me a house? I'm going to build* ***you*** *a house, and one more thing: I've been waiting for the man after my own heart, the king who would rule out of the priestly heart of ministering to Me, and I've found him. It's you, and MY Son, the Messiah, will come through your lineage and He will sit on YOUR throne. He will forever be known as the son of David.*

The closest analogy I can think of for this statement would be God looking at me and my life and saying, *the Messiah is coming and His last name will be Russell.* I cannot even imagine the honor of God taking my name, and this same reality struck David as he received this promise.

The implications of one man's impact on the eternal God are mind-boggling.

David's desire to not rest until God rested is made clear in Psalm 132 when Solomon at the dedication of the temple called on God to remember his dad and his extreme sacrifice and dedication to see God's house established on the earth. Standing at the dedication of the temple, Solomon in essence said, "There is only one card

I can play that will invoke the favor of God: my dad and his life."

> LORD, remember David and all his afflictions. (Ps. 132:1)

Many times in the Word we are called to remember God, but how many times do we see someone calling on God to remember a man, his life, his dedication and sacrifice? What is it about men and women's choices that can so impact God?

It was this thought that began to lay hold of me in August 2013 as I considered my son, his legacy, and the fact that I had one moment in history to go all in, to contribute everything I had toward God's dream of dwelling on the earth. I knew that this would honor God, but it was also honoring the memory of my son. **I wanted to live a life that moved God and that would be remembered before Him forever.**

I believe there are moments and specific actions that live forever. Mary of Bethany took her whole life's inheritance, a very costly spikenard, broke its alabaster bottle, and poured it all over Jesus. Jesus said that what this woman had done would be told as a memorial to her. It would forever live before the throne. I believe this desire of David's also pulled eternity down and will always be remembered.

I felt in some ways that Nash's death awakened me out of complacency and released a desperate cry to go all out for God, to not waste time and energy on things that don't have eternal impact.

"All his afflictions" — Psalm 132 directly connects all of David's many afflictions with his desire to find a dwelling place for God on the earth. We must realize that this desire of David's didn't start when he was king, but was the driving force of his whole life beginning in his teenage years in Bethlehem. He caught a vision of this, and it governed his life. Once this vision laid hold of him, I believe it awakened the rage of Satan, which manifested through his brothers, Saul, and everything that followed.

Once this vision gets hold of your life, all of hell begins to tremble. I believe it was this vision of the dwelling place that provoked the rage of Satan to release many afflictions in David's life. Beginning with rejection and jealousy from his own brothers, he experienced many involuntary troubles, including jealousy and a murderous spirit from his father-in-law, and being hunted as a fugitive. There were demonic afflictions, family afflictions, and personal afflictions.

> **For Your sake** I have borne reproach; shame has covered my face. I have become a stranger to my brothers, and an alien to my mother's children; **because zeal for Your house has eaten me up, and the reproaches of those who reproach You have fallen on me**. When I wept and chastened my soul with fasting, that became my reproach. I also made sackcloth my garment; I became a byword to them. Those who sit in the gate speak against me, and I am the song of the drunkards. (Ps. 69:7–12)

David understood that it was zeal for God's house that provoked reproach, shame, rejection, etc. He made a vow in his early days, and this vow stayed with him through all of his life. Solomon declared that this vow laid hold of David's life and it included an all-out war on comfort, rest, and slumber until God's desire was made manifest.

> He **swore** to the LORD, and **vowed** to the Mighty One of Jacob: "Surely I will not go into the chamber of my house, or go up to the comfort of my bed; I will not give sleep to my eyes or slumber to my eyelids, until I find a place for the LORD." (Ps. 132:2–5)

David declared war on the "American Dream" so that the Heavenly Dream would be manifested in his generation. David decided that he would not carry on with life as usual while God was not dwelling in his generation.

I spent from August 2013 all the way to December 31, 2013, burning with this word in my heart, knowing that in light of my son's passing, I had one moment to go all out, laying hold of the deepest longing in God's heart: the union of heaven and earth, God and man (see Revelation 21:3 and Ephesians 1:9–10). I know that in the same way Solomon stood on his dad's shoulders, there is deep connection between my son's life in heaven and my life here on earth.

Psalm 132 gave permission to my heart to pour out everything to see God's longing established on the earth. I felt as if Nash was cheering me on to give my strength, pain, and desire — to put it all on the line. Knowing that brought comfort to my heart.

I preached this message at the last session of our ministry's Onething conference on December 31, 2013, and called forth thousands of Davids who would lay hold of God's heart and labor for dwelling places to be established all over the earth. I watched as God marked thousands of young people with a burning desire to do whatever was necessary to see God's presence restored in their city and nation in this generation.

Psalm 1

Blessed is the man
Who walks not in the counsel of the ungodly,
Nor stands in the path of sinners,
Nor sits in the seat of the scornful;
But his delight is in the law of the LORD,
And in His law he meditates day and night.
He shall be like a tree
Planted by the rivers of water,
That brings forth its fruit in its season,
Whose leaf also shall not wither;
And whatever he does shall prosper.

The ungodly are not so,
But are like the chaff which the wind drives away.
Therefore the ungodly shall not stand in the judgment,
Nor sinners in the congregation of the righteous.

For the LORD knows the way of the righteous,
But the way of the ungodly shall perish.

5
Psalm 1: The Foundation of Psalm 2

2014 IS THE YEAR OF THE REVELATION of intercession." This is the phrase the Holy Spirit spoke to me on January 2, 2014, in Mexico City. Literally two days after preaching Psalm 132 at the Onething conference, God was giving me a new mandate. He immediately spoke to me about Psalm 2 and how He was going to begin to release greater understanding and revelation of the power of intercession.

Though God spoke immediately to me about Psalm 2, the Lord directed me to Psalm 1 and, for the first time, connected these two psalms in a very real and direct way. Being a man of the Word, I've always loved Psalm 1 because of the obvious blessings that come upon someone's life when they meditate in the Word. However, what I began to see in Psalm 1, as it related to Psalm 2, is that there are two conversations and value systems that are vying for our attention: the value system of the world and the value system of heaven contained in the Word of God. The Lord made clear to me that we will either come underneath the leadership of God's words and experience the blessings contained in them, or we will rage against them, seeking to throw them out and break them off our lives, our culture, and our generation. This blessing specifically plays out in the ministry of intercession, because the word we receive from God will come back out of us to God, thereby releasing His power into the earth.

The truth in Psalms 1–2 has been one of the most profound and strengthening revelations God used to navigate my heart through the grieving process after losing Nash. I believe they are essential for this generation, and I would venture to say that I believe these two chapters may be among the most important in these days, in which we are seeing a global rage against God, His leadership, and His Word. In short, it's the call to a deep intimacy with the Word of God that, in the days of chaos and storm, we would come forth and cry out for our inheritance.

There is a deep connection between Psalm 1 and 2. What we find in Psalm 1 is the blessing that comes upon a person who makes concrete decisions to find the Word as his or her number-one source of life, joy, delight, comfort, and strength, versus the opinions of the day.

If anything has happened through these last few years since Nash's passing, it's that I've become dependent to my core on the Word of God. The psalms give language to a grieving, clinging heart like nowhere else in the Word of God, and they have given exact articulation to the deepest words of my heart. I do not know where I would be without them. One of my main purposes in writing this book is to highlight the fact that the Word of God is the greatest comfort there is. I'm grateful for books that share people's testimonies of how they went through a horrible tragedy and came out on the other side. There even may be a sense of gratitude to the Lord for carrying them through it. But sadly I don't hear that much on how the Word of God, and specific chapters and realities, strengthened them.

This is the gold that a generation is needing in order to navigate through not only personal storms that test their faith, but culture-altering storms that I believe are about to break out on this generation and cause many to fall away. We desperately need the Word as an anchor for the soul. In Psalm 119, David gives us amazing insight on the power of the Word to carry us through affliction.

> This is my comfort in my affliction, for Your word has given me life. (Ps. 119:50)

> Before I was afflicted I went astray, but now I keep Your word. (Ps. 119:67)

> It is good for me that I have been afflicted, that I may learn Your statutes. (Ps. 119:71)

> Unless Your law had been my delight, I would then have perished in my affliction. (Ps. 119:92)

Junk happens to everyone, unbeliever and believer alike. Death, tragedy, loss, and trauma are experiences common to everyone living, and no one is immune or exempt from them. However, the believer has the chance in trials to turn that suffering into glory and into an eternal reward.

> For our light affliction, which is but for a moment, **is working for us** a far more exceeding and eternal weight of glory. (2 Cor. 4:17)

When we take God's Word and cling to it as our only hope, strength, joy, and delight, God rewrites our story and carries us through the worst of storms. This book is about the five psalms that carried me through my darkest night. These are Bible chapters, not self-help techniques, coping mechanisms, or other forms of comfort, but the Word of God. Our generation desperately needs a deeper life in the Word to navigate life's storms, as well as global and end-time storms that are on the horizon.

Before we look at Psalm 2, let's look at God's prescribed way to avoid the rage and resistance to Him and His Word that it describes. That way is found in Psalm 1: by breaking through the pages into a living encounter with the Man Jesus Christ and finding our sole delight, joy, and mediation in His Word.

Psalm 1 begins with the word *blessed*. David is letting us know that the person who wants a blessed life must make three concrete choices regarding what people and opinions they will not engage with, so that they may engage fully engage with something/ SOMEONE else.

> Blessed is the man walks not in the counsel of the ungodly, nor stands in the path of sinners, nor sits in the seat of the scornful; but his delight is in the law of the Lord, and in His law he meditates day and night. (v. 1–2)

The blessing and favor of God come upon the person who understands the deceptive and progressive nature of sin, and completely avoids the people, the words, and the sentiment around it. Look at the progression in verse 1 from walking to standing to sitting.

My friend Matt Candler was preaching a message on this recently and stated that the walking, standing, and sitting can be likened to the way we act in front of our televisions when we are looking for something to watch. Flipping the channels can be likened to walking. Momentarily stopping on a channel, holding the remote ready, can be likened to standing; and putting down the remote and sitting back on the couch can be likened to sitting. Whatever or whomever we are walking with today, we will be standing with the next day and ultimately end up sitting in agreement with the following day. The human heart slowly acclimates to whatever it is tolerating. It never starts off fully entrenched but is like the frog in the kettle, gradually becoming acclimated to deeper levels of sin and deception.

There are so many believers these days who are walking, standing, and sitting in places, and with people, that are in direct opposition to the blessed life of meditation on God's Word. You are either going to be shaped by the words of this culture or by the words of God, but either way: words will shape your life.

The psalmist's call is to stay away from three areas of temporary delight and give ourselves to the eternal delight of meditation on the Word of God. **I'm convinced with all my heart that one of the primary breakdowns in our nation is the church's lack of pleasure and delight in the Word of God.** When David uses the word *law*, he is referring to the only Word of God he had. Whether it's the first five books of the Bible or the whole written Word of God, the fact remains the same: the Word is meant to change us. The Word of God has stayed on the pages and has not gotten into our mouths, and therefore has not brought change to our interior lives, our faith, love, and hope. This lack begins in our church leadership and trickles down to the very fabric of our faith.

We are living in a culture that is at war with the Word of God. The authority of the Scripture is being undermined and challenged left and right in our seminaries, churches, and homes. Even from well-meaning believers, I'm hearing phrases like, "That guy is such a Biblicist," or "a literalist." Their statements imply that we don't need to be so narrow minded as to take the Word of God literally (as if it means what it says) and that we shouldn't be so lost in the Bible that we miss Jesus. I read on Twitter today: "The Bible itself says that Scripture is useful. It doesn't say much more. It comes from God and is useful."

The Bible has become in many people's eyes a book of suggestions instead of the inspired, written Word of God. Truth has become relative — whatever a person deems it to be. We as a nation are told we have no right to alienate another group, and their set of "truths," with our set of truths. The Word that was meant to stand over us and speak to us has been reversed, and now we are the ones standing over the Word, interpreting it as we like to fit our lives. This is being fueled by leaders and pastors who are emboldening this mentality through the messages and lifestyles that they live. Respected Christians are actually shying away from the Word of God en masse because of fear of man and wanting the respect (and the money) of the people. That's why I believe that Psalm 1 is the answer for the church in this hour. The psalmist begins by stating that there are three areas we must abstain from if we seek a blessed life, and then takes us into the answer: meditation and delight in His Word.

I believe that the first step forward for the church is a rediscovery of delight in the Word of God. The primary way we do this is through meditation, which is simply speaking, vocalizing, and engaging with the Word of God. We must begin to see the Word not as an historic book but a conversation that God has begun and wants us to respond to. The very word *meditation* means in Hebrew to ponder while speaking to oneself (see *Strong's Exhaustive Concordance*, #7878, *siach*). God's remedy for you is the simple truth that the Word has to get off the pages and get into your mouth, because it will be your own mouth that will be your deliverance (see Revelation 12:11). This truth is very profound, as we will see later in Psalm 2. God's Word written on our hearts is the only thing that will endure the coming storm, delivering us from the counsel of the ungodly, the path of sinners, and the seat of the scornful. Can you feel the urgency to go a different way and begin to sit before His Word, hear it, and speak and sing it back to Him?

I love the fact that the psalmist says, "Meditate day and night." I believe this is prophecy of God raising up day-and-night prayer and worship all over the earth, when people will sit, walk, and stand in prayer rooms, living rooms, bedrooms, church rooms and work rooms all hours of the day to speak and sing God's Word back to Him and see rapid change. The very charge that God gave Joshua in Joshua 1:7–8 was to take courage and meditate in the law day and night, as the very source of strength and courage to take the land promised.

Most of us think of meditation and prayer as separate activities, but to me, they are one and the same. Hans Urs von Balthasar, the twentieth-century Swiss theologian, says in his book *Prayer*, "Prayer *is* dialogue, not man's monologue before God," and that "a particular language *is* spoken: God's language" (Balthasar, *Prayer* [San Francisco: Ignatius Press, 1986],14). Meditation is thinking and praying God's Word back to God. God speaks His Word, and it moves our heart. We then speak the Word back to God, and it moves His heart. This is why Psalms 1 and 2 are so intricately connected. We receive the Word in Psalm 1. We ask for our inheritance in Psalm 2. It's all revolving around words inspired by God.

As we will see in Psalm 2, when nations are raging and the Word is being thrown off, God's answer and primary battle strategy is intercession. Intercession is simply telling God what He tells us to tell Him, but it's not merely parroting it back to Him. It begins with us sitting before the Word of God and through long and loving meditation, the Word moves past our minds and begins to rearrange the furniture of our interior life. "Faith comes by hearing, and hearing by the Word of God" (Rom. 10:17). The degree to which we hear His Word will be the degree to which He hears ours. John 15:7 makes it clear that when we abide in His Word, He gives us the desires of our heart. This is because through meditation, His desires become our desires, and He will always answer that which began with Him. One of my favorite statements from Mike Bickle is, "God speaks the word and it moves our hearts. We then speak the word back to God and it moves His heart."

Immediately after describing this blessed person who delights and meditates in God's Word, Psalm 1 then lays out what these blessings look like.

> He shall be like a tree planted by the rivers of water, that brings forth its fruit in its season, whose leaf also shall not wither; and whatever he does shall proper. (Ps. 1:3)

Trees speak of stability, durability, and rootedness, of being unmovable, constant. We see that the ones who meditate will remain stable and durable and constant through the changing of the seasons. This imagery is picked up time and time again. In Jeremiah's day, God breaks down the crisis to the difference between ones who do this (meditate) and the ones who don't. He terms the ones who don't do this as "cursed" and the ones who do it as "blessed."

> "**Cursed** is the man who trusts in man and makes flesh his strength, whose heart departs from the LORD. For he shall be like a shrub in the desert, and shall not see when good comes, but shall inhabit the parched places in the wilderness, in a salt land which is not inhabited.
>
> "**Blessed** is the man who trusts in the LORD, and whose hope is the LORD. For he shall be like a tree planted by the waters, which spreads out its roots by the river, and will not fear when heat comes; but its leaf will be green, and will not be anxious in the year of drought, nor will cease from yielding fruit." (Jer. 17:5–8)

These trees aren't just planted, but are planted by rivers, which speaks of a constant source of water, nourishment, and sustainment from the Lord. These trees will bring forth fruit in season, which means the fruit will come forth, just give it time. These trees will not wither even in the toughest of seasons, they will not fear, and they will not be anxious, but will continue to yield fruit in the worst of seasons and will prosper in everything they put their hands to. I don't know about you, but this is the kind of man I want to be. Justin Rizzo, a worship leader here in Kansas City, has written a great song based on this psalm. The lyrics are, "I want to be unmovable, unshakable; so let my roots go down deep, unmovable, unshakable in You. I want to be like a tree planted by the streams of living water" (Rizzo, "Tree" [Forerunner Music, 2007]). I can't think of a better prayer to pray than this one.

On January 2, 2014, God began to call me into Psalms 1–2 in a very clear and direct way. I felt urgency from the Holy Spirit that in the midst of our own grieving over the loss of Nash, I must come out of any counsel, or path, or conversation that would cause my heart to accuse God and His leadership in my life and in the life of my family. Even though I didn't understand what was going on, I knew that the Holy Spirit was calling me to a renewed love for His Word, because this would be the only safe place in the days to come. As I set my heart before Psalms 1–2 in 2014 and 2015, God anchored my heart, my emotions, and my thoughts in Him. At times I could literally feel my root system in God going deeper and deeper, and I knew that He was calling me and my family to be a tree of protection, safety, and shade for so many others who would be walking through similar storms in the days ahead.

Psalm 2

Why do the nations rage,
And the people plot a vain thing?
The kings of the earth set themselves,
And the rulers take counsel together,
Against the LORD and against His Anointed, saying,
"Let us break Their bonds in pieces
And cast away Their cords from us."

He who sits in the heavens shall laugh;
The LORD shall hold them in derision.
Then He shall speak to them in His wrath,
And distress them in His deep displeasure:
"Yet I have set My King
On My holy hill of Zion."

"I will declare the decree:
The LORD has said to Me,
'You are My Son,
Today I have begotten You.
Ask of Me, and I will give You
The nations for Your inheritance,
And the ends of the earth for Your possession.
You shall break them with a rod of iron;
You shall dash them to pieces like a potter's vessel.'"

Now therefore, be wise, O kings;
Be instructed, you judges of the earth.
Serve the LORD with fear,
And rejoice with trembling.
Kiss the Son, lest He be angry,
And you perish in the way,
When His wrath is kindled but a little.
Blessed are all those who put their trust in Him.

6
Psalm 2: Inheritance

PSALM 2 HAS DRIVEN ONE MASSIVE POINT deep into my heart as I've walked through the last five years of grieving the loss of our son: **the greatest places of our warfare are to become the greatest places of our inheritance.** This psalm is all about Satan's final attempt to steal from Jesus His inheritance, His throne, and His people.

The psalm begins with nations that are raging, and in the middle of it all, we find Jesus hearing from the Father: *You see those nations that are raging against My plan? Ask Me for them, and I'll give them to You as Your inheritance.*

> Why do the nations rage, and the people plot a vain thing? The kings of the earth set themselves, and the rulers take counsel together, against the LORD and against His Anointed, saying, "Let us break Their bonds in pieces and cast away Their cords from us." (Ps. 2:1–3)

In Psalm 2, David in a prophetic encounter is getting undone over the state of humanity in the generation of the Lord's return. He begins this psalm with the question, "Why?" He can't comprehend what he's seeing. He can't wrap his mind around the overt hostility and rage in the human heart against God and His Word, and he's even more blown away by the plan that's in their hearts to overthrow God. He calls it "vain," meaning it is useless and futile to think that the created can remove the Creator, yet these people are unified and energized to try to do that. It's absolute insanity at its fullness. It's like building a sand castle all day on the beach, thinking it will stand forever, just to have a small wave come in and take down in five seconds what took all day to build.

The spirit displayed in Psalm 2 is alive and well in these days — we see an open, defiant, bold celebration of things God clearly calls evil. Our generation has concluded that they don't have to weep and repent for their sin, but can celebrate it and export it. We are seeing a hyper-grace generation that has taken the glorious message of our free, full acceptance by God through Christ as meaning that God is in full agreement with whatever we choose to do, because He's a loving father. But we must love God on His terms, not on the terms our culture gives.

David is prophetically witnessing a global, unified conspiracy of nations and peoples with their most influential players (kings and judges) declaring war on the Father and the Son and His Word. We must understand that if you don't come underneath the word of Psalm 1 and find delight in its boundary lines and restraints, then you will begin to see God's Word as cords and bonds that restrict your self expression and freedom to rule yourself. This is the cause of rage. Rage is Satan's primary emotion; it has been since his exit from heaven. Specifically the Bible states that during the Great

Tribulation (that three-and-a-half year period before the Lord's return) Satan is going to lose his authority in the heavens, and his first emotion and response will be rage — rage against God, His Son, His people, and His Word. This rage will cause Satan to invest his resources, power, and ability to deceive into the man the book of Revelation calls "the Beast," the "man of sin," or "the Antichrist." Rage erupts when the revelation strikes you that you're not God and that you're not strong enough or smart enough to do what you want to. It's actually rage against God and His standards laid out in the Word. Your life, your sexuality, your family and children, your nation and its economy coming underneath the standards of the Word of God will elicit rage, if you are not already in agreement with that Word. To the nations, peoples, kings, and judges who continually and willfully choose themselves and each other's words over God's Word, He will send strong delusion (2 Thess. 2:11), and because of their hatred of the truth, God will give them what they want and the king they want. You will either love the Word or you will hate it.

The "rage" that David is witnessing is targeted towards the Father and the Son, His Word, and His choosing of the nation of Israel. Again, this rage has been expressed through the centuries but will find its full expression in the days preceding the return of Jesus, as Satan seeks to annihilate the Jewish race from the planet. The nation that God chose through Abraham, Isaac, and Jacob has long been the object of Satan's rage. If God would have chosen any other nation or people, that nation and people would have become the target. Satan rages because God chooses. We will see this on full display on a global scale as the days before Jesus' return come. Zechariah is very clear that all nations will surround Jerusalem, but the people they seek to remove will end up being their ruin (Zech. 12:3; 14:2).

One can view Psalm 2 like a four-act play with four distinct actors. In the first act, we see raging nations. God wants to take His messengers into the heart and bitterness of this first scene to connect us with His plan, His heart, and His zeal for His people. After the first act the curtains close, and when they reopen, we are taken away from the horizontal viewpoint of seeing nations rage and taken up to the throne where the Father is sitting. God doesn't leave David (or us) in the despair of the first scene, but takes us up into the place of hope and security, showing us that our Father is seated in the heavens far above all of the activity below and that He is actively, aggressively engaged with what is going on. God wants His people to feel the delusion, vanity, and demonic opposition to God for what it is, but at the same time, He does not want us to engage in this battle from a horizontal, human level, but calls us up into the heavenly realms to join Jesus in His place of perspective and engagement.

> He who sits **in the heavens** shall laugh; the Lord shall hold them in derision. Then He shall speak to them in His wrath, and distress them in His deep displeasure: "Yet I have set My King on My holy hill of Zion." (Ps. 2:4–6)

It's as if act 1 closed, and when act 2 opens we see the Father seated in the heavens and we hear His perspective concerning the nations that are conspiring and plotting against Him and His Son. It's important to note that He is "in the heavens." This heavenly perspective is of utmost importance as we venture into the days ahead. We must come out of the Fox News/CNN evaluation of the day and connect to the heavenly, eternal, sovereign confidence of the Father and to His plan to give all nations to His Son, beginning with Zion.

In verse four we watch the Father seeing the same thing as David but having a completely different response: He laughs. This is one of most terrifying statements in the Bible, and this laugh the most terrifying laugh in history; it's one you don't want to find yourself on the other side of. The Father views these raging nations, kings, and rulers, and in a mocking tone laughs at them, speaks to them that they are not going to succeed, and distresses them with a loud, resounding eternal declaration: "I HAVE SET MY KING ON MY HOLY HILL OF ZION!" My paraphrase of His declaration goes something like this: *There is one King, and His name is Jesus; and there is one city, and its name is Zion (Jerusalem). You kings will not rule, because I've already ordained and openly declared the destiny of My Son as King over all the earth. No devil, demon, antichrist, man, or woman will be able to change My mind or to overpower or outwit Me.*

I love the different faces of the Father. I love the Father who embraces us in our most vulnerable and weakest places. I love the Father who is compassionate, tender. But I believe we need to see and feel the heart of the Father revealed in Psalm 2, who is intensely engaged against anything that steals from His Son's inheritance. The Father loves the Son.

Right now, Jesus is enthroned as King at the right hand of the Father in heaven. This was settled at His ascension, and it's been the place from where He's ruled for the last 2,000 years. **He is enthroned, and He is going to be enthroned.** He is ruling in heaven, and He is going to be ruling from that hotly disputed hill in Jerusalem that the nations are fighting for supremacy over today.

He is seated right now far above every principality, power, might, and dominion in this age and in the next. The fullness of this verse is about Jesus' coronation as King in Jerusalem when He returns.

In this declaration, we feel the Father's anger toward the nations and His deep love and commitment to His Son and to His people. How is the Father going to speak to the nations? He's going to do it through the mouths of His messengers who will proclaim, "Humble yourselves, kiss the Son, and get into alignment with His plan, or you will be crushed."

Act 2 closes and when act 3 opens, we find the Son standing before the Father in light of the Father's declaration over Him. David is eavesdropping on the greatest conversation ever: the Father talking to the Son in the eternal counsels about how the Son will inherit and receive the raging nations and peoples. This is the crux of the whole psalm.

What is God's answer? What is His methodology for responding to the first scene of rage? How is the Son going to become king? What is the rule of His kingdom? How does He rule? **These questions are so profound because they contain the secret for how we today, as the first scene of Psalm 2 is emerging, can respond to the Lord.**

> "I will declare the decree: the LORD has said to Me, 'You are My Son, today I have begotten You. Ask of Me, and I will give You the nations for Your inheritance, and the ends of the earth for Your possession. You shall break them with a rod of iron; You shall dash them to pieces like a potter's vessel.'" (Ps. 2:7–9)

Where do we find Jesus when all the chaos, confusion, and craziness are erupting? We find Him praying. **His answer to the rage is intercession**. This is honestly surprising to me. He's the King. The Father has already given the nations to Him and boldly declared that those nations don't win, but His Son wins. Jesus comes forth in the place of intercession and is going to simply, yet profoundly make clear to us the ministry of intercession: *I'm going to declare back to the Father what He has declared over Me.* David is coming in on the back end of this conversation, and what he hears is Jesus speaking to the Father, "I will declare the decree." *I will tell Abba what He told Me to tell Him.* This is so simple yet so profound. Why is telling Father what He told us to tell Him the means by which we receive our inheritance? The Father is initiator, the One who begins the conversation by declaring realities about His Son — who He is to the Father, and what His inheritance is. This is where intercession begins.

Intercession begins with the Father declaring over our lives His affection, His love, His emotions toward us as His sons and daughters. The declaration, "You are My Son," is going to be the revelation of the end-time prayer movement that brings the church out of shame and into intimacy and faith. His affections are what break down our walls of defense. We become open to His words and His promises over our life because we know He is good and we can trust Him. This revelation is being released all over the earth right now in a profound way as the Father's love is being poured out in the hearts of His children. The thing I'm afraid of is that this revelation becomes separated from a response of prayer and intercession. I love the healing aspect of the Father's love, but His love heals us to bring us forth out of shame and fear and into a place of intimacy and faith to believe all God has spoken over our lives, our families, our churches, our cities, and our nations. Jesus reminded us of what the Father said about His own house: "My house shall be called a house of prayer" (Mark 11:17).

The revelation of "You are My Son" is not only about affection, but is about inheritance.

> "Ask of Me, and I will give You the nations for Your **inheritance,** and the ends of the earth for Your possession." (Ps. 2:8)

The Father openly declares His love for His Son and then states something like, *Son, I love You and I have an inheritance for You:* ***the nations****. Do You see those nations that are raging? Ask Me for them, and I'll make them Your inheritance.* As I said earlier, the Holy Spirit spoke to me in this season when Psalm 2 became clear, that ***my greatest places of warfare are to become my greatest places of inheritance.***

I don't know about you, but these last few years have been really hard, and most of the people I'm talking to are saying the same thing. There has been much warfare, loss, and setback, but the Father is calling His people forth to join His Son in receiving His affection over us and His inheritance for us.

As we receive the Father's declaration over our lives, we begin to see them in this age, and ultimately in the next, through His eyes. It is when we begin to see as He sees, that prayer emerges. Once you see your inheritance, you boldly ask for it. You start to ask like you never have before, because you know it's yours. The Father told Jesus that the nations are His, but He must ask for them. **What is it about asking that reveals the nature of the kingdom?** Asking connects your heart to His, your dreams to His, your life to His; asking causes you to be formed into a vessel that can manifest the fulfillment of the answer.

The Father then tells the Son to ask Him for the nations. Why does He have to ask? What does asking do? We are seeing in this eternal conversation that the Father has ordained that **intimate intercession** will be the basis of receiving inheritance. Their exchange in the throne room is to become the pattern for our own lives, families, churches, cities, and nations. Asking the Father for what He said He wants to give us is the basis for receiving it. The asking unites our hearts to His, conforming us into the image of His Son, humbling us, healing us, transforming us, and all the while releasing our inheritance to us. God is brilliant!

The very nations that are raging will become the Son's inheritance as He asks for them. All nations will come under the leadership of Jesus Christ. His will and desire will govern the fabric of every society in the entire world. This is the Father's promise to His Son.

This revelation has already begun to, and will continue to, explode across the earth. Prayer and worship is breaking out and going viral in every tribe, tongue, people, and nation. Worship is agreement with who God is. Prayer is agreement with what God said He would do. It's all about agreement. The Father is escorting the church out of the "Accusation Room" and into the "Agreement Room." This will only increase in the coming days as nations awaken to the glory and power of agreement with heaven for the in-breaking of heaven and the return of Jesus Christ.

What is your inheritance? I spent the majority of 2014–2015 with the word *inheritance* resting on me, and I began to wrestle over that question. What is my inheritance in Christ? Ephesians 1 lays out many spiritual blessings we've received in Christ, but I began to ask specifically who or what is my inheritance? As I've wrestled over this, I've come to these present conclusions. Psalm 16:5 declares that "The Lord is the portion of my inheritance." Not only is He my inheritance — I'm His inheritance. For me, my marriage is my inheritance; my children are my inheritance; my family is my inheritance; my calling is my inheritance; my city and nation are my inheritance.

It was in the middle of this season of asking for my inheritance that a friend of mine sent a dream that has given more hope and strength to my heart than just about anything else has in regards to the death of my son, what he means to me, his legacy, and my inheritance from this day forward. We named our son Nash after Daniel Nash, the intercessor for Charles Finney. He was an integral part of Finney's success. For a seven-year period they teamed up through private praying and public preaching, and saw arguably one of the greatest moves of mass salvations ever in this nation. My wife and I were so impacted by his secret life of intercession, we wanted to name our son after him and see a spirit of prayer come upon our boy. After Nash's passing, I had constantly cried out to God for a storyline that made sense of all of this, to help me know what to give myself to, as well as call others to. This dream gave that to me. My friend wrote:

> *In the dream, I found myself in a city with many intercessors and prophetic people I knew and have met around the U.S. The city was built like a castle and had a medieval feel to it. The enemy had laid siege to the city, and there was great fear among the people. I was gathering up these people and instructing and training them in warfare and various tactics. Suddenly you (Corey) walked in with Allen Hood following behind you, and we locked eyes and said, "These are the days that we have been living for."*
>
> *You (Corey) began to speak with great authority, boldness, and courage to the people. You shouted to them and told them that they must not flee, but to do everything that they can to stand. As you finished speaking, the spirit of prophecy fell upon me and I said,* ***"Corey! For every one voice of awakening that God is releasing in America, He is releasing seven voices of intercession that will prepare the way for the coming revival!"***

Again, I shouted to you and said, "Corey! For every one voice of awakening that God is releasing in America, He is releasing seven voices of intercession that will prepare the way for the coming revival!"

I continued on and said to you, "God gave Lou Engle the Nazarites in this nation, but He is now giving you the "Nasharites" in this nation. You will raise up a generation of Nashes, voices of intercession, which will outnumber the voices of awakening. My Spirit blows through these young Nasharites like a gust of wind, but you will take them and turn them into houses of prayer. The mark of the Nasharites is that they themselves will be called "Houses of Prayer."

These "Nasharites" are an intercessory army that God is raising up all over the earth. They are nameless and faceless. They are hidden from the eyes of men, but are beloved in the eyes of God. Their weapons are holiness, prayer, fasting, and declaring the Word of God with a perseverance that will not be denied. They will win the war in the heavenlies that will see the breakthrough of God come to homes, families, churches, cities, and regions with the Word of God. They will battle with the forces of darkness, suffer setbacks and loss, and some will even lose their life or loved ones' lives, but they will not shrink back. They will keep pressing, pushing, reaching, striving, praying, withstanding until every promise that God made is fulfilled in their generation. They will be sustained by intimacy with Jesus, fellowship with the Holy Spirit, and the embrace of the Father. God's Word of promises and declarations and decrees will be the loudest.

The comfort, strength, vision, and courage this dream has given to me in the midst of these last five years is huge. My inheritance is that God will raise up one hundred million revival intercessors across the earth, who, though they are not known by men, are known in heaven. As it relates to the nations, my prayer is that God would raise up Nasharites in every tribe, tongue, people, and nation.

> "'You shall break them with a rod of iron; You shall dash them to pieces like a potter's vessel.'" (Ps 2:9)

This is the fruit of these Nasharites' intercession: the release of the power of God on His Word; revival breaking out and destroying every opposition in its path. The fullness of this reality will take place when Jesus returns and utterly destroys all opposition with the power of His Word, but since the Day of Pentecost and the outpouring of the Holy Spirit, we have seen seasons when God's Word dashes sin, sickness, and Satan to pieces like a piece of pottery. The second part of this verse is intense as we see Jesus' leadership and dominion over the nations at His coming, and His rule as King during the Millennium. This is how He will rule the nations.

Jesus' death, resurrection, and ascension now bring us into union and partnership with Him in hearing from the Father and asking for the nations. I absolutely love that Jesus shares this glorious honor of intercession with His people and that we can partner with Him in seeing His inheritance come forth in the nations. His "rod" will come out of the mouth of the church, destroying the power of the evil one in the earth.

In Revelation 2:26–27, Jesus declared to the church of Thyatira that His reward to those who overcame was that He would give them the power over the nations that His Father gave Him. He quotes Psalm 2:

> "And he who overcomes, and keeps My works until the end, to him I will give power over the nations — **'He shall rule them with a rod of iron; they shall be dashed to pieces like the potter's vessels'** — as I also have received from My Father."

As Jesus received it in Psalm 2, He now shares His authority with the church. Many people only see the ultimate fulfillment of this reality without understanding that God has given us and will give us a significant measure of this same reality in this age through the gospel. The early church in the book of Acts used Psalm 2 to interpret their context, believing that God would do what He said in Psalm 2 for them. In Acts 4, Peter and John had just been released from prison after healing the man at the Beautiful Gate. The Sadducees and other religious leaders threatened them; but at the end of the day, what could these leaders say against a once-lame man who was now standing before them? They couldn't do anything to Peter and John, so they let them go. This is such an interesting time in the early church. There seemed to be a crack in the dam of resistance to the gospel, and the two pillars, Peter and John were now set free. Consider the mindset of the early church once these apostles returned to them. The early church used Psalm 2 as the very backdrop for the crisis they were in, and through Jesus' death and resurrection, they prayed that God would put the rod of His Son in the mouth of the church.

> So when they heard that, they raised their voice to God with one accord and said: "Lord, You are God, who made heaven and earth and the sea, and all that is in them, who by the mouth of Your servant David have said:
>
> > 'Why did the nations rage, and the people plot vain things?
> > The kings of the earth took their stand,
> > And the rulers were gathered together
> > Against the Lord and against His Christ.'" (Acts 4:24–26)

They bring Psalm 2 into their context and begin to follow the scenes laid out in it to a tee. It seems that they understood Psalm

2 as the model prayer for the Messianic Kingdom beginning with Jesus' resurrection.

> "For truly against Your holy Servant Jesus, whom You anointed [enthroned], both Herod and Pontius Pilate, with the Gentiles and the people of Israel, were gathered together [nations raging] to do whatever Your hand and Your purpose determined before to be done. [Sovereign Father] Now, Lord, look on their threats, and grant to Your servants that with all boldness they may speak Your word, by stretching out Your hand to heal, and that signs and wonders may be done through the name of Your holy Servant Jesus." And when they had prayed, the place where they were assembled together was shaken; and they were all filled with the Holy Spirit, and they spoke the word of God with boldness. (Acts 4:27–31)

In this prayer, the early believers follow the Psalm 2 model. They interpret raging nations as Herod, Pilate, Gentiles, and people of Israel. They interpret the installing of Jesus as King as the anointing on His ministry and His resurrection from the dead, and they interpret the Father's sovereign position to mean that He was the one who, by His hand and purpose, determined everything to be done.

They seem to establish the first two scenes (of Psalm 2) in their prayer, and when it comes to the third scene of Jesus' intercession, they enter into intercession asking for the rod of God to be released through them by the anointing of the Holy Spirit. The boldness of proclamation, the healing anointing, and signs and wonders would serve as the rod that would dash all opposition into pieces. The Word of God in power is the rod that rules. God immediately answered this prayer by shaking the house, filling them with the Holy Spirit, and releasing a fresh anointing and unction on the Word of God. After this prayer, the early church's impact rose dramatically as great power, great grace, and great fear fell upon the region.

This Nasharite army can be found several places in the Word of God. It's going to be an intercessory army of hidden men and women, young and old, who will see great power released in the earth through prayer and fasting. Revelation 12 is the picture of where this praying army will go. In this passage, we see war break out. Reading this will quickly remind the reader of Daniel 10 and the connection between Daniel's prayer and fasting, the dislodging of evil powers over Persia, and the release of angelic ministry. In Revelation 12, the war results in Satan losing his authority in the heavenly realm and being cast to the earth. This is good news for the heavenly realm, yet things become more intense on the earth as Satan, filled with rage, comes after God's people. This is the power of prayer and fasting: it actually causes that which is hidden in the spirit realm to lose its power by manifesting in the natural realm. It can feel like things are getting worse, but they are actually getting better, because now you know who your enemy is, and you can break its power by declaring the Word of God. I believe this weapon of prayer and fasting will become a very dear weapon for the end-time church.

> **And war broke out in heaven**: Michael and his angels fought with the dragon; and the dragon and his angels fought, but they did not prevail, nor was a place found for them in heaven any longer. So the great dragon was cast out, that serpent of old, called the Devil and Satan, who deceives the whole world; he was cast to the earth, and his angels were cast out with him. Then I heard a loud voice saying in heaven, "Now salvation, and strength, and the kingdom of our God, and the power of His Christ have come, for the accuser of our brethren, who accused them before our God day and night, has been cast down. And they overcame him by the blood of the Lamb and by the word of their testimony, and they did not love their lives to the death." (Rev. 12:7–11)

Revelation of the Son's intercession is going to fill the end-time prayer movement in a deep way. We are already beginning to see it explode across the earth as God brings together the prayer and the missions movements. Churches and ministries all over this nation are beginning to prioritize prayer like never before.

I preached Psalm 2 every weekend from about June 2014 to June 2015, calling forth intercessors, whom I termed Nasharites. watched the Lord mark young and old, male and female, from many nations with the spirit of prayer in a remarkable way. Many times the Lord would sovereignly sweep into a room, and a burden of prayer would come on people. It was an amazing time and so comforting to my heart to see my son's legacy touching the nations with the spirit of prayer for revival. These ministry times were dear because I felt my son close to me. As I told his story, I felt a strange connection to him and partnership with him in ministry. I remember one night specifically in Singapore as I preached on Psalm 2 and then shared the story of our son and the call of the Nasharites. To me the message didn't seem that strong, judging by its reception and sense of authority, but as soon as I shared Nash's story and gave an altar call, I was blown away by the release of the spirit of prayer upon the thousand people attending. I was truly in touch with God's zeal to set intercessors on the wall for revival in the nations.

During this time I was continually reminded of another dream shared by a friend who had seen a dynamic connection continuing between my son and me. I knew I had set Nash on my arm like a seal (Song 8:6), and that the effect I was having now as I labored in ministry was part of his legacy, fueled by my enduring love for my son. He is alive, and in a sense the two of us are in partnership for the benefit of the church, to raise up many Nashes who will intercede before the throne just as Jesus the Son intercedes before His Father. That praying army will be my inheritance, and it will also be my son's. This season brought so much healing and comfort to my heart, as I saw the purpose of my son's life brought forth in great clarity.

Psalm 91

He who dwells in the secret place of the Most High
Shall abide under the shadow of the Almighty.
I will say of the LORD, "He is my refuge and my fortress;
My God, in Him I will trust."

Surely He shall deliver you from the snare of the fowler
And from the perilous pestilence.
He shall cover you with His feathers,
And under His wings you shall take refuge;
His truth shall be your shield and buckler.
You shall not be afraid of the terror by night,
Nor of the arrow that flies by day,
Nor of the pestilence that walks in darkness,
Nor of the destruction that lays waste at noonday.

A thousand may fall at your side,
And ten thousand at your right hand;
But it shall not come near you.
Only with your eyes shall you look,
And see the reward of the wicked.

Because you have made the LORD, who is my refuge,
Even the Most High, your dwelling place,
No evil shall befall you,
Nor shall any plague come near your dwelling;
For He shall give His angels charge over you,
To keep you in all your ways.
In their hands they shall bear you up,
Lest you dash your foot against a stone.
You shall tread upon the lion and the cobra,
The young lion and the serpent you shall trample underfoot.

"Because he has set his love upon Me,
therefore I will deliver him;
I will set him on high, because he has known My name.
He shall call upon Me, and I will answer him;
I will be with him in trouble;
I will deliver him and honor him.
With long life I will satisfy him,
And show him My salvation."

7
Psalm 91: Protection

Psalm 2 painted a vivid scene of the warfare, chaos, and confusion that the enemy will wage around the deepest places of inheritance. From 2013–2015, I felt the enemy's rage, his warfare, against my deepest inheritance: my family. It was Psalm 2 that gave me the simple yet profound response: intimacy-based intercession. I didn't have strength to do a lot in that season, but there was one thing I could do — I could sit before the Father, hear and receive His affection, and ask for my inheritance in Him.

Around June 2015, as the summer began, I set my heart to focus on who God is. I've found the attributes of God to be a great strength and comfort, specifically the eternity of God. When meditating on the eternity of God, I find that my afflictions in this age, no matter how intense, are light when compared to eternity. Meditating on the eternity of God lifts me above the temporal storms and gives me an eternal perspective. Over the past few years, in the wake of Nash's death, this truth has sustained and strengthened my heart massively.

In Psalm 90:2, Moses writes, "From everlasting to everlasting, You are God." He has no beginning and He has no end; He is the everlasting "I AM." I began to meditate on passages like this one and prayer-read through the following Psalms. Seemingly by accident, as I began to read and pray through Psalm 91, God began to arrest my heart, and this psalm that I thought I was very familiar with gripped me in a way that it had never had before. I knew that God was throwing another lifeline to my family and me, to sustain and strengthen us for the next season. Honestly, the summer and fall of 2015 would prove to be the most difficult time that we would walk through in this five-year season following Nash's death, but at the point where the enemy would try his hardest to separate, destroy, and kill our family, God emphasized Psalm 91. He gave us a hiding place, and from there we could navigate through the storm.

As the Holy Spirit emphasized Psalm 91, four truths became very evident. These were revolutionary to me.

1. God is committed to providing protection, provision, and immunity.
2. The psalm's promises are conditional, given to the ones who make Him their dwelling place versus their "crisis ATM."
3. I must memorize this psalm and declare it to God, over my heart, and against the devil.
4. The backdrop of the psalm is intense: pestilence and death.

I was absolutely blown away by what God said He would do for the people who make Him their dwelling place and who set their love upon Him. I began to see the conditions of Psalm 91 as a call to make Him my dwelling place. The psalmist declared that

God would deliver that person, cover that person both at night and in the day. He would give His angels charge over them to carry them and protect them. At the end of Psalm 91 in verses 14–16, God steps in and makes a seven-fold commitment to the person who has "set his love upon Me" (v. 14).

1. **He will deliver them**
2. **He will set them on high (the place of revelation)**
3. **He will answer their prayers**
4. **He will be with them in trouble**
5. **He will honor them**
6. **He will satisfy them with long life**
7. **He will show them His salvation**

The Lord was very clear with me about memorizing this passage and making it the priority of my prayer life for the next couple of months. He told me to declare it back to Him over my life and family, and against the Devil.

Shortly after God drew me into this psalm, He gave me a real-life prophetic picture of its reality. In Kansas City, we are used to tornadoes and the threat of tornadoes coming through our city. One evening that summer, our whole family was outside playing and hanging out when storm clouds began to gather, which is, honestly, one of the most fascinating, beautiful, and terrifying things to see. They move so fast. To see the dark clouds meet the bright clouds, to see lighting strikes, and then to see funnels drop down some twenty to thirty miles away — it's absolutely beautiful. Our family was literally caught up in the scene transpiring before our eyes when all of a sudden, the most obnoxious sound began. It started off in the background and continued. I was subconsciously tolerating it until it stopped, but after about a minute, I began to realize that it wasn't going to. It was then that an earth-shattering revelation hit me: **this is a siren warning us that a tornado is getting close and we need to seek shelter as soon as possible.** (You would have thought that the fact that no one else was outside would have been enough, but it wasn't.) We quickly transitioned to the basement, and though the tornado went just north of us, the Lord began to speak to me regarding Psalm 91.

I became deeply aware in that moment of the reality of storms that are breaking into this nation and this generation, and more specifically, the storm that had and was continuing to come through our family. I also became deeply connected with the fact that sirens are going off as clear indicators of this storm. We are seeing national storms, sexual storms, theological storms, and family storms gathering; the things coming out of our court rooms, bedrooms, and churches are clear indicators of the danger — alarms are going off.

The family storm was one that we were feeling in a very personal way. The death of Nash had released an earthquake in our family, exposing every fault line. In seasons like this, unresolved issues that were just annoyances become exacerbated to tens on the Richter scale. They say that the percentage of marriages to not survive the death of a child is astronomical, and I honestly understand that. I have deep compassion for marriages that don't make it through these seasons. When these kinds of devastating events hit your life, everyone goes into survival mode, doing all they know to just stay alive. For me, it became a messianic mission of carrying my family through this dark night. For my wife, it was doing her best to carry on through her day but just wanting to go to sleep once evening came. For my oldest daughter, it was looking to friends to fill that void, and for my middle daughter, it was taking on the false burden of being the best sister-mom to our youngest daughter.

It's human nature to look to something or someone as a place of security, but God brings all of the false securities to the surface so that He can draw us to the only One who can shelter us, protect us, and provide for us in these storms. **He alone is our dwelling place**. I knew that God would carry us through the storm despite all of our running, escaping, and fear-motivated tendencies, and would reveal His glory in us and through all of this.

I had wrestled for years over the fact that Jesus compared the days preceding His return to the days of Noah. My first prayer CD, done in 2004, was titled *Days of Noah*. I was invited to speak at a conference in Montana, and the name of the conference was "Days of Noah." On the flight out there, I began to tell the Lord how unfair it was that Noah preached for one hundred twenty years and no one got saved but his family, and immediately the Holy Spirit spoke back to me: "But his family got saved. And in the last days, I'm going to raise up arks of safety, called families, who will go through the worst of storms and come out on the other side and make fresh covenant with Me." His words had always stayed with me, and now I felt I truly understood them, because I had lived them. I believe God will take many families through storms like ours and bring them through to the other side. These families will be a witness to the power of God to preserve and deliver His people through the darkest of nights.

Prophecies of the last days are filled with predictions of the breakdown of the marriage and family units. Paul saw there would come a day that marriage would be outlawed (1Tim. 4:3). What do you think would cause this to come about? Could it be the fact that the institution doesn't mean anything anymore, due to the prevalence of divorce (in the church and outside of it), homosexual marriage, "open marriages," and the like?

In Second Timothy 3, Paul wrote in the middle of a long list of last-days trends that people would be "disobedient to parents" (v. 2). We cannot fully grasp the significance of the breakdown of the family unit that will come when adults despise the generation that raised them and children won't even listen to their parents anymore, partly because their words don't mean anything, due to the hypocrisy of their own lives.

While it's clear that marriage and family is under an all-time assault, the Lord has given us a powerful prophetic promise that this will not be the only thing going on with families in the last days.

> Behold, I will send you Elijah the prophet before the coming of the great and dreadful day of the LORD. And he will turn the hearts of the fathers to the children, and the hearts of the children to their fathers, lest I come and strike the earth with a curse. (Mal. 4:5–6)

Before the Lord returns, He is going to release a prophetic spirit that will manifest in homes and in the midst of families. I'm convinced that the greatest anointing is one that turns a heart, and God will release this anointing before He returns. The days are coming when Christian fathers will no longer sacrifice their children on the altar of ministry, money, or themselves, but will sow themselves into their natural and spiritual children to see the heart of a generation turn back to them. By God's power, marriages and families will stay together in the wake of tragedies and will become "arks of safety" for the final generation. Because these family units will be so essential, I'm not surprised the enemy has unleashed an all-out war on them. I know he unleashed it on us.

This is why I believe Psalm 91 is so important for us in this hour. It gives us a clear prescription for safety: **make Him your dwelling place**. More than just a crisis ATM, who we run to in times of emergency, we must begin to make Him our primary source of joy, entertainment, comfort, and peace. The psalmist makes it clear that there is a place of immunity, or protection and provision, and it's in Him.

In one sense, we are "in Him," and He is "in us," but there is a big difference between having access to something or someone and actually accessing it or them. Many believers are content with the fact that they said a prayer at an altar inviting Jesus into their hearts, and are living their lives investing their time, money, and energy into themselves, disconnected from Him. The call to make Him your dwelling place includes living an intentional life of abiding in Him, fellowshipping with the indwelling Spirit, obeying His small and large promptings, quickly running from anything or anyone who disturbs your conscience, and seeking to live in unity and intimacy with Him.

I believe that an active engagement with the indwelling Spirit and with others who are seeking to do the same is one of the greatest ways to survive these current storms, as well as navigate through the coming ones.

I want to tell you that we didn't immediately see the fruit of this abiding. There were many painful and dark nights in this time. Things actually got more painful in the summer and fall of 2015, yet it was in this season that walls each of us had built began to crack, and it was in this season that the slow, painful journey toward healing really began. After the first two years of basically survival, God had begun the restoration. Looking back at when things were at an all-time painful place, we see that our weak reaching to abide in Him actually hid us, carried us, and strengthened us. The "fruit" of our abiding in Him is the fact that we are here, that we didn't quit, and that we love each other and are filled with hope for a great future.

Friend, I don't know what your story is or has been, but I want to call you to deeply abiding in Him, drawing on Him, and living in Him. As you seek to do this, He promises you that He will deliver, protect, and carry you through the darkest of nights.

Psalm 18

I will love You, O Lord, my strength.
The Lord is my rock and my fortress and my deliverer;
My God, my strength, in whom I will trust;
My shield and the horn of my salvation, my stronghold.
I will call upon the Lord, who is worthy to be praised;
So shall I be saved from my enemies.

The pangs of death surrounded me,
And the floods of ungodliness made me afraid.
The sorrows of Sheol surrounded me;
The snares of death confronted me.
In my distress I called upon the Lord,
And cried out to my God;
He heard my voice from His temple,
And my cry came before Him, even to His ears.

Then the earth shook and trembled;
The foundations of the hills also quaked and were shaken,
Because He was angry.
Smoke went up from His nostrils,
And devouring fire from His mouth;
Coals were kindled by it.
He bowed the heavens also, and came down
With darkness under His feet.
And He rode upon a cherub, and flew;
He flew upon the wings of the wind.
He made darkness His secret place;
His canopy around Him was dark waters
And thick clouds of the skies.
From the brightness before Him,
His thick clouds passed with hailstones and coals of fire.

The Lord thundered from heaven,
And the Most High uttered His voice,
Hailstones and coals of fire.

He sent out His arrows and scattered the foe,
Lightnings in abundance, and He vanquished them.
Then the channels of the sea were seen,
The foundations of the world were uncovered
At Your rebuke, O LORD,
At the blast of the breath of Your nostrils.

He sent from above, He took me;
He drew me out of many waters.
He delivered me from my strong enemy,
From those who hated me,
For they were too strong for me.
They confronted me in the day of my calamity,
But the LORD was my support.
He also brought me out into a broad place;
He delivered me because He delighted in me.

The LORD rewarded me according to my righteousness;
According to the cleanness of my hands
He has recompensed me.
For I have kept the ways of the LORD,
And have not wickedly departed from my God.
For all His judgments were before me,
And I did not put away His statutes from me.
I was also blameless before Him,
And I kept myself from my iniquity.
Therefore the LORD has recompensed me
according to my righteousness,
According to the cleanness of my hands in His sight.

With the merciful You will show Yourself merciful;
With a blameless man You will show Yourself blameless;
With the pure You will show Yourself pure;
And with the devious You will show Yourself shrewd.
For You will save the humble people,
But will bring down haughty looks.

For You will light my lamp;
The LORD my God will enlighten my darkness.
For by You I can run against a troop,
By my God I can leap over a wall.
As for God, His way is perfect;
The word of the LORD is proven;
He is a shield to all who trust in Him.

For who is God, except the LORD?
And who is a rock, except our God?
It is God who arms me with strength,
And makes my way perfect.
He makes my feet like the feet of deer,
And sets me on my high places.
He teaches my hands to make war,
So that my arms can bend a bow of bronze.

You have also given me the shield of Your salvation;
Your right hand has held me up,
Your gentleness has made me great.
You enlarged my path under me,
So my feet did not slip.

I have pursued my enemies and overtaken them;
Neither did I turn back again till they were destroyed.
I have wounded them,
So that they could not rise;
They have fallen under my feet.
For You have armed me with strength for the battle;
You have subdued under me those who rose up against me.
You have also given me the necks of my enemies,
So that I destroyed those who hated me.
They cried out, but there was none to save;
Even to the LORD, but He did not answer them.
Then I beat them as fine as the dust before the wind;
I cast them out like dirt in the streets.

You have delivered me from the strivings of the people;
You have made me the head of the nations;
A people I have not known shall serve me.
As soon as they hear of me they obey me;
The foreigners submit to me.
The foreigners fade away,
And come frightened from their hideouts.

The LORD lives!
Blessed be my Rock!
Let the God of my salvation be exalted.
It is God who avenges me,
And subdues the peoples under me;
He delivers me from my enemies.

You also lift me up above those who rise against me;
You have delivered me from the violent man.
Therefore I will give thanks to You, O LORD, among the Gentiles,
And sing praises to Your name.

Great deliverance He gives to His king,
And shows mercy to His anointed,
To David and his descendants forevermore.

8
Psalm 18: Deliverance

> The **pangs of death** surrounded me, and the **floods of ungodliness** made me afraid. The **sorrows of Sheol** surrounded me; the **snares of death** confronted me. In my distress, I called upon the Lord, and cried out to My God. (Ps. 18:4–6)

As the summer of 2015 progressed into the fall, a deep groan began within me for deliverance for my family. The last two years had been marked with deep grief, deep pain, loneliness, and our inability to articulate what was going on inside of us. Though I sought to keep bringing the five of us together as a family, it seemed more and more that everyone just wanted to go to their individual islands and "do their thing." I tried to take our oldest daughter with me a lot that summer to travel. I wanted to connect our hearts and get her in the presence of the Lord, as well as bring comfort to my own heart that was hurting.

In late summer to early fall of 2015, I began to get drawn into Psalm 18. My prayer went from primarily the prayer for protection out of Psalm 91 and became a more desperate cry for deliverance, specifically out of Psalm 18. Our family needed a breakthrough, a serious breakthrough. I didn't know what that meant, but I knew something had to shift. Coming out of the Psalm 91 season of abiding in God as our refuge, dwelling place, and protection, I began to search psalms that had the element of the Lord being our refuge, strength, and protection; this is what initially led me to Psalm 18. However, as I began to meditate on it and see David's progression from praising God for his deliverance to then describing the deliverance, a deep and desperate cry began to arise in me for our deliverance. Psalm 18 gave language to a cry in my heart when I didn't have language. This was David's psalm of victory and praise after God delivered him from Saul, as well as all his enemies. It was a psalm of great praise for God's deliverance in his life. **God delivered him from the most impossible of situations.**

Though I hadn't experienced the full deliverance yet, I became confident in God's desire and ability to deliver our family from the scourge that had passed through and been tearing us apart. I felt pressed on every side like David. I felt the pangs of death, the floods of ungodliness, the sorrows of Sheol, and the snares of death confronting me. I felt the Lord calling me to do what David did when surrounded with these four horrible realities: **cry out to Him.** Just as the children of Israel "groaned" under the bondage of slavery, and the groan reached God, I began to groan and long and cry out for deliverance, praying that my groan would reach His ears.

I want you to know that your cries, tears, and groans do not go unnoticed by God but are very dear to Him and awaken His activity in your life. Take your pain, your brokenness, your weaknesses and pour them out on the only One who can do something about it. Cast your cares upon Him, for He cares for you (1 Pet. 5:7).

> He heard my voice from His temple, and my cry came before Him, even to His ears. (v. 6)

I knew that my cry was reaching Him and that I was awakening

His fierceness as the "warrior God" to come down and to intervene in our lives and bring deliverance. I had never thought like this before, but I literally began to call on the "angry God" of verse 7 to come down in glory and power. There was a righteous anger growing in me, an insistence on seeing God "flex" in our family and bring restoration. I longed for a shift in me, in us, that would bring us forth into our destiny.

> Then the earth shook and trembled; the foundations of the hills also quaked and were shaken, **because He was angry**. Smoke went up from His nostrils, and devouring fire from His mouth. (vv. 7–8)

"Because He was angry" consumed me. Through prayer we are saved from our enemies (v. 3), who are also God's enemies. I wanted His anger manifested against the enemies that had sought to destroy our family. Since Nash's passing, the enemy had tried to take our family out through depression, fear, shame, isolation, lies, accusations, and distrust. I wanted God to release His power in a manifest way.

> The LORD thundered from heaven, and the Most High uttered His voice, hailstones and coals of fire. He sent out His arrows and scattered the foe, lightnings in abundance, and He vanquished them. **Then the channels of the sea were seen, the foundations of the world were uncovered**. (vv. 13–15)

"The foundations of the world were uncovered" — what happens when God's voice thunders into your life and everything that was covered and hidden is fully exposed? God's voice breaking in always signifies a changing of the seasons, and I knew that something was about to be confronted and destroyed. It is terrifying to think of God bringing everything to light by the power of His voice, yet I longed for it and for His deliverance.

> He sent from above, He took **me**; He drew **me** out of many waters. He delivered **me** from **my** strong enemy, from those who hated **me**, for they were too strong for **me**. They confronted **me** in the day of **my** calamity, but the LORD was **my** support. He also brought **me** out into a broad place; He delivered **me** because He delighted in **me**. (vv. 16–19)

In these four verses, we see *me* or *my* twelve times. David, in the middle of great warfare and conflict, cried out to God; the heavens opened, God descended and thundered His voice, uncovering everything that surrounded. He came in like a Navy SEAL team rescuing a prisoner of war, descending in a helicopter to pull the POW out of the war prison.

The enemy sought to take advantage of a weak and vulnerable season in David's life. In the same way Satan sought those "opportune times" to come at Jesus (Luke 4:13), so David's enemies confronted him in the day of his calamity. For me, this was a season the enemy had come with all the vengeance of hell against me, my wife, and my children to steal, kill, and destroy. It was an all-out assault, and it was messy. In many ways, during the end of that summer, I felt like I and my family were in a prison camp surrounded on every side by darkness.

But I'm here to tell you that He broke in. He came from above and drew me, my wife, and my children out of many waters, delivering us from those principalities and powers that hated us, that sought to kill us in our most vulnerable hour of our life. What was the main motivation for His deliverance in my life? — His delight in me, in us.

Do you have any idea how much He takes delight in you and

your reaching for Him in your weakest and most vulnerable seasons of life? This so stirs His heart and awakens the "warrior God" to intervene on your behalf.

I believe that many people have felt like David in Psalm 18, with pangs of death, sorrows of Sheol, floods of ungodliness, and snares of death surrounding them on every side. Whether this assault came in through the loss of a child, like it did for us, or the loss of a spouse, or some other loss that shook everything to the core, I believe God has given us Psalm 18 as a battle cry — no matter how impossible the situation looks around us, we can lift our eyes and our voices to God and cry out, and He will make our enemies His enemies and break in with great power and deliverance.

God isn't just into delivering you; He wants to turn your deliverance into a testimony that releases authority to destroy the works of the devil in other people's lives. He wants to take you from just making it to pursuing your enemies and destroying them and their effects in others' lives and families.

Look at the confidence and authority that was released in David's life through seeing God's deliverance:

> For You will light my lamp; the Lord my God will enlighten my darkness. For by You, I can run against a troop, by my God I can leap over a wall. (vv. 28–29)

David declared in confidence that God would light his lamp and end the current season of darkness. He declared that by and with God, he could overcome impossible odds.

> It is God who arms me with strength, and makes my way perfect. He makes my feet like the feet of deer, and sets me on my high places. He teaches my hands to make war. (vv. 32–34)
>
> Your gentleness has made me great. (v. 35)

God's gentleness with us in our weakest and most vulnerable seasons is the **only** reason we make it and fulfill our destiny.

> I have pursued my enemies and overtaken them; neither did I turn back again till they were destroyed. I have wounded them, so that they could not rise; they have fallen under my feet. For You have armed me with strength for the battle; You have subdued under me those who rose up against me. You have also given me the necks of my enemies, so that I destroyed those who hated me. They cried out, but there was none to save; even to the LORD, but He did not answer them. Then I beat them as fine as the dust before the wind. (vv. 37–42)

Though chapter 18 begins so grim and dark, it ends with David destroying the very enemies that almost took him out. The opponents that surrounded David are now being hunted by David. He is resolute in destroying them, wounding them, beating them, crushing them, and putting his feet on their necks. The deliverance he received when he cried out to God will not be afforded to them when they cry out to God.

I believe with all my heart that God wants to awaken the cry for the "warrior God" to intervene in our lives and families. What almost took you out will prove to be the training tool of the Lord to teach you how to fight and to overcome. In the place of desperate intercession, of clinging to God, He will manifest His breakthrough.

As our family moved into the fall of 2015, we began to see the Lord break in, break through, uncover, and deliver us out of the schemes and plans of the enemy. There was a pivotal shift in how my wife and I were relating in our brokenness. From day one after "the call," I had become gripped with fear, which led to control and trying to manage everyone. This changed our relationship from one of husband/wife to more of father/daughter. We lost each other in all of this, and we didn't know how to break out of the cycle of my fear playing on my wife's shame. God began to uncover the issue and deal with it in a very painful, yet liberating way. He enabled me to give up my control and fear and brought forth a deep love for my wife. It was through this that she, for the first time in a long time, saw my love for her and the Lord's love for her; it freed her heart in many ways.

This was a breaking point season for us emotionally and relationally, and it became the season when He broke in and delivered us from the enemy.

Psalm 23

The LORD is my shepherd;
I shall not want.
He makes me to lie down in green pastures;
He leads me beside the still waters.
He restores my soul;
He leads me in the paths of righteousness
For His name's sake.

Yea, though I walk through the valley of the shadow of death,
I will fear no evil;
For You are with me;
Your rod and Your staff, they comfort me.

You prepare a table before me in the presence of my enemies;
You anoint my head with oil;
My cup runs over.
Surely goodness and mercy shall follow me
All the days of my life;
And I will dwell in the house of the LORD
Forever.

9

Psalm 23: Shepherd

On January 23, 2016, I had a profound encounter with the Lord through Psalm 23, and I knew that God was bringing forth a fresh revelation of Himself. I was to focus that year on the face of Jesus as Shepherd.

The day before, my wife and I had been scheduled to join my good friend Allen Hood in Connecticut for a ministry trip. He was already in New York City with his son, but we were coming from Kansas City. Early that morning, Dana woke up very sick; she was throwing up, and it became clear that she was not going to be able to join me on this trip. I got ready and started heading to the airport alone. On the way, I called the airline to let them know that I needed to cancel Dana's ticket. Because I'm a frequent flyer, I usually am able to get to a customer service representative within seconds, but it took about twenty minutes before I got a person on the phone. When they picked up, I asked why it had taken so long, and they said that one of the biggest snowstorms in recent history was about to hit the East Coast. Hundreds of flights were being canceled. I told him that I was flying through Washington, DC, and the guy explained that I would be lucky to get out of there. It was likely the airport would be shut down for two to three days, which was the duration of my trip. All of a sudden, I pictured my wife at home terribly sick with three kids and me stuck in an airport for three days unable to get home, and I freaked out. I called the pastor of the place I was going and told him the situation; he was very kind and gracious to release me from the trip. I went ahead and canceled the trip and headed home. (Allen wasn't as nice to me. He was stuck in Connecticut for three days after the conference because of that snowstorm.)

A small part of me was relieved to be home for a weekend. I had traveled more the previous two years than ever before and was feeling some exhaustion setting in as the new year came. I was looking forward to being with my girls while my wife rested. At the same time, I was feeling for Allen and felt really bad for having to leave him in Connecticut to carry the preaching load of the weekend. The past two years had been intense in many ways, and this whole situation of letting my best friend down really shook me. I came to an emotional point where I couldn't handle it anymore. It seemed, in some ways, that this was the straw that broke the camel's back.

The next morning, still feeling pained over leaving Allen on his own, I got up early to be with the Lord. We had just had our Onething conference and one of the highlights was Audrey Assad's song "I Shall Not Want." I decided to pull that song up and begin to think about the phrase, "I shall not want."

I opened my Bible to Psalm 23 and turned that song on, and one of those special, rare moments ensued. As I began to read through the Psalm with the song in the background, it was as if Jesus walked into the room, placed His hand on my heart, and began to slowly speak each phrase of Psalm 23 over me, causing every word to explode off the page and into my heart.

I was literally undone by the presence of God. It was as if I had never read this chapter before, as every phrase left me overwhelmed at the power and glory of Jesus as my Shepherd. I knew that the revelation of Jesus as Shepherd was going to be the facet of Jesus I was to focus on over the next year, and I immediately connected this to our journey of walking through grief since the loss of my son. The intensity of this experience seemed to last about forty-five minutes, and for the first time in three years, I felt holy vulnerability—I would let Jesus shepherd me. I literally sensed Him asking if He could shepherd me, and I told Him *yes*. I had come to the end of my rope trying to manage and "fix" my family and my life and keep everything going, and I knew in that moment that He was relieving of me of my duties and was going to bring me into a deep place of rest in Him. Though I wasn't in touch with it at the time, once I got "the call" from Dana that Nash passed, and I wasn't there for the first day and a half, I began to put on myself a burden that God was not putting on me; it was the burden of carrying everyone, since I hadn't been there to see him dead. I'd felt responsible to be strong, to carry everyone else; now I felt the Lord telling me that He was going to carry me. He actually told me that He was going to MAKE me lie down in green pastures this year. I had always imagined that verse as something like me lying in a field of grass and Jesus playing a violin, or me just sitting down, drinking a tea, and relaxing. But the tone and force of "make you lie down" resounded inside of me, bringing comfort and fear at the same time. I felt His force, zeal, and resolve to bring me to a place of divine rest, of submission to His will so that He could minister to things deep within me that had transpired over the past several years since Nash's death.

In this encounter with Psalm 23, several thoughts and verses began to rush into my mind. One of the clearest ones was Revelation 7 and the Lord's treatment of those who had endured the Great Tribulation. The Lord told me that what He is going to do for those coming out of the Great Tribulation, He will do for those who come out of tribulation seasons in this life. I knew that He was going to do these things for me.

> Then one of the elders answered, saying to me, "Who are these arrayed in white robes, and where did they come from?" And I said to him, "Sir, you know." So he said to me, "**These are the ones** who come out of the great tribulation, and washed their robes and **made them white in the blood** of the Lamb. Therefore they are **before the throne of God**, and **serve Him day and night in His temple**. And He who sits on the throne **will dwell among them**. They shall neither hunger anymore nor thirst anymore; **the sun shall not strike them, nor any heat**; for **the Lamb** who is in the midst of the throne **will shepherd them and lead them to living fountains of waters**. And **God will wipe away every tear from their eyes**." (Rev. 7:13–17)

Look at heaven's treatment of those who come out of the Great Tribulation! It's like war heroes returning from battle, and all of heaven celebrates, rejoices, and gives them high honor in the immediate presence of God. The Lamb in the midst of the throne shepherds them and leads them to living fountains of water, and God Himself personally addresses the tears in the eyes of His people.

As this passage began to flood into my heart, I immediately began to sense heaven's honor for those who endure tribulation seasons. I could imagine the angels shouting, "These are the ONES!!!" These ones washed their robes in the blood, removing the stains of the last season. They are given access to the throne and are commissioned to serve day and night in the temple, having nearness to God. They no longer have to endure the elements like they did before, and the Lamb shepherds these ones.

Even in heaven, a process of recovery takes place. In Revelation 6, the martyrs who are asking God for justice are given new white robes while they wait. And in this passage, they aren't restored instantaneously when they exit the Great Tribulation. They are led to living fountains of waters, and they still have tears in their eyes, which means that the stains, memories, deficiencies, and pain connected to the last season still remain, and God addresses these things.

Another thing that was highlighted to me is the fact that the Shepherd shows up after tribulation. These are heroes in heaven, but they still need shepherding to recover from the last season. This thought alone may have been the most impactful and freeing revelation that I have received in these last five years. If this is what these "greats" of history needed from God, then I could let down my guard and submit to His restoration of my soul and washing of me. It hit me like a ton of bricks: they had no idea the impact of their choices and what it meant to God, and for the first time, I felt such an honor. I also realized that everyone needs healing and restoration, and it's not just for the "broken ones." This allowed me to feel honored while at the same time realize and accept my need for healing and restoration.

During this encounter, I literally felt Jesus walking me to the living fountains of waters and baptizing me, washing away tears, and pouring His love into me. His grace brought me to a place of beautiful vulnerability — I trusted enough to let Him shepherd me.

It became very clear to me that Psalm 22 precedes Psalm 23 for a good reason. Psalm 22 begins with, "My God, My God, why have You forsaken Me?" Those who go through seasons when they cannot sense God's presence anywhere may reach out to anything and anyone for security and stability, yet God will not allow it to happen. These tribulation seasons expose the fault lines in our lives, marriages, families, and ministries, shaking everything that can be shaken, driving us to the one place of safety and security: the Shepherd. We go from, "My God, where are you?" to "My God, You are my Shepherd, I shall not want." It's in the shaking that He brings us to Himself as the sole fulfiller of every longing and desire. Something happens in you when you can't find God in the midst of the most painful and vulnerable places — desperation is birthed; you look desperately for Him.

These Psalm-22 seasons of "My God, My God, where are you?" are meant to cause us to come to rest in Him alone. When these seasons come, some people run to other things to medicate and anesthetize the pain, like alcohol, drugs, and illicit relationships, but they soon discover that the security and healing they are looking for is not found in these places. He alone is the sole source of comfort, healing, and peace.

What is it about the revelation of God as Shepherd that is so important to those coming out of tribulation seasons? I believe that this specific face of Jesus is going to be emphasized in a great way in the generation before His return.

> The LORD is my Shepherd; I shall not want. He makes me to lie down in green pastures; He leads me beside the still waters. He restores my soul; He leads me in the paths of righteousness for His name's sake. Yea, though I walk through the valley of the shadow of death, I will fear no evil; for You are with me; Your rod and Your staff, they comfort me. You prepare a table before me in the presence of my enemies; You anoint my head with oil; my cup runs over. Surely goodness and mercy shall follow me all the days of my life; and I will dwell in the house of the LORD forever. (Ps. 23)

This psalm has to be the most famous chapter in the whole Word of God. Most unbelievers know it. I see the whole thing or portions of it in most houses hanging on walls; I read it on greeting cards; I hear it at funerals. We've been surrounded with this psalm for as long as we've been alive, and I believe that God wants to knock the overfamiliarity off so that we can come into a deeper revelation of our need for a Shepherd, the process He takes us through during hard times, and the purpose He wants to fulfill in and through us.

Coming out of the tribulation season of Psalm 22, we are brought into a divine encounter with the Shepherd, and He fulfills our needs. He makes us lie down, putting us into a divine season of being brought to a place of dependence on Him. I've heard it said of shepherds and sheep that one of the ways a shepherd will deal with a sheep that gets lost or wanders is to use the rod to guide it, so the sheep stays close to the shepherd and cannot wander too far. A sheep kept close like this discovers the Shepherd's voice.

Though I hadn't "wandered off" or "lost my way," I did feel as though God was putting me into a place of divine constraint/discipline. I was actually relieved at the thought of stopping for a season. I just didn't know how to get there. I told the Lord to set it up, and that I would be all in.

Before we look at the psalm, I want to share three reasons why I believe God is highlighting this psalm in these days:

1. To minister restoration to those who have come through, or are coming through, tribulation seasons
2. To give understanding so that we trust He is with us in a current season of tribulation
3. To commission a new breed of shepherds who are called to give leadership in the church during coming days of glory and crisis

The Shepherd "makes" us lie down, so that we are living dependently on Him, and He leads us to still waters. It's in this place that He restores our souls. As I was praying through the reality of still waters one day, it dawned on me that you can only see your reflection in still waters. God sets up seasons and scenarios that cause us to come to rest, look down in the untroubled waters, and go on a journey of self-reflection.

> As in water face reflects face, so a man's heart reveals the man. (Prov. 27:19)

In these still waters the restoration of our souls takes place. God is a restorer. He is a redeemer, and no matter the trauma, pain, or loss you've experienced, it's not the end of your story. God personally leads us to the place where our souls are restored from the last season. He washes our minds, our emotions, and our bodies in His healing river.

Many times the journey is hard as we discover ourselves and see the toll of the survival years on our psyche, our emotional chemistry, and our physical bodies. This is the place of self-reflection, but the whole aim of God in this season is His glory, not a preoccupation with ourselves.

He leads us in paths of righteousness not for our comfort's sake, or our reputation's sake, but for "His name's sake" (v. 3). What is a "**path of righteousness**"? It can be a difficult road, a narrow road, but it's the sure road to everlasting life, and God will not lead another way. We see this as He takes His favorite ones through the valley of the shadow of death. God sets up scenarios in our lives that we must walk through. He doesn't allow us to run, and He doesn't allow us to go around or bypass them. He puts a regulator on the accelerator of our lives and causes things to move at a slow, arduous pace. Hours feel like days; days feel like months; months feel like years; and years feel like decades. At the time I'm writing this, it's been four years since our son passed away, but it has felt like a ten- to fifteen-year season. If anything has become very clear over these last years, it is the reality that God is into the process. He doesn't think it a waste of time to take His favorite ones through the slow process of changing them through the two-steps-forward, one-step-back journey to maturity.

At the end of Exodus 2, we see "it happened in the process of time that the king of Egypt died. Then the children of Israel groaned because of the bondage, and they cried out; and their cry came up to God because of the bondage" (v. 23). For 430 years, the children of Israel had been slaves in Egypt; all of a sudden the season shifted, and a deep groan that had grown over centuries began to arise to the throne. God moved on their behalf by releasing a deliverer who He had been preparing through forty years of mundane shepherding to shepherd the people of Israel out of Egypt and into the promises of God. God took a prince of Egypt out of Egypt and to the back side of the desert, and emptied him of all of his own abilities so that God could show Himself strong through him.

God is into the process. Being honest, I would say that up until these last four years, everything had for the most part come easy for me. I experienced a sovereign, instantaneous salvation and deliverance from all drugs. Prayer and studying the Bible came easy to me. I never knew a time when I didn't encounter God in the Bible and prayer. After I was saved, preaching became as natural as breathing. Though the development and content took time, I've always had an ability to communicate and articulate what God was speaking to me.

But then my son passed away, the floor fell out from under us, and every deficiency, weakness, insecurity, fear, inability, and need for control became glaringly clear. The process began. I faced my powerlessness for the first time in my life. Why in God's preparation of a messenger and message does He first have to bankrupt you in order to fill you, and why doesn't He speed that season up?

> Yea, though I walk through the valley of the shadow of death, I will fear no evil; for You are with me. (Ps. 23:4)

It's not just the shadow of death, but death itself that we walk through. When death itself casts its shadow on your life, and you feel that you are on the brink of not making it, everything that you dreamed for your life is also not going to make it. Have you ever been there, friend?

And yet God causes you to walk through it, releasing one overwhelming revelation in the midst of this season: He is with me. No matter how close I get to death, how dark it gets, how hopeless it feels, I refuse to be overcome by my surrounding circumstances, knowing that He is with me. He is able to shepherd me through the worst of nights because He went before me through the valley of the shadow of death. He trusted His Father when He hung suspended between heaven and earth, becoming the sin offering for the world. He trusted His Father when He was in Sheol, trusting the Father would not leave His soul there but would raise Him up, showing Him the path of life. We can trust Jesus to lead us through because He's been there before, and He came out on the other side. Therefore, He's going to bring us through to the other side. **Friend, you can trust Him. He's been there.**

You can trust His leadership. David came to a revelation that when the Shepherd uses His rod and staff it's actually for the purpose of bringing true comfort. Many people will allow Him to "lead" them as long as it doesn't infringe too much on their personal comfort, reputation, and vision, but as soon as the Shepherd begins to bring His people under the rod, many believers bail. The shepherd's rod is used to both protect the sheep from predators as well as guide wayward sheep. This represents both God's discipline of His children and defense of them against enemies.

I'm so grateful for the revelation of sonship that is sweeping the Body of Christ in these days. It is a revelation of God as a good, loving, compassionate Father who embraces us in our weakest and most vulnerable places; who fully and freely bestows upon us His free grace, love, and mercy; who gives us the family name, the family seal, and the family inheritance. However, one of the key signs of our sonship and the "proofs" that we are sons is our endurance through the chastening and discipline of the Father.

In Hebrews 12, the writer makes very clear the reality of chastening, the purpose of chastening, and the fruit of chastening. (I would highly recommend Bob Sorge's book *The Chastening of the Lord: The Forgotten Doctrine* for more on this.)

> If you endure chastening, **God deals with you as with sons**; for what son is there whom a father does not chasten? But if you are without chastening, of which all have become partakers, then you are illegitimate and not sons. Furthermore, we have had human fathers who corrected us, and we paid them respect. Shall we not much more readily be in subjection to the Father of spirits and live? For they indeed for a few days chastened us as seemed best to them, but He for our profit, that we may be partakers of His holiness. Now no chastening seems to be joyful for the present, but painful; nevertheless, afterward, it yields the peaceable fruit of righteousness to those who have been trained by it. (Heb. 12:7–11)

David in Psalm 23 is looking back at God's dealings in his life — His discipline and use of the rod — and confidently declares that His rod brought comfort. It led David to a place of peace, dependence, rest, and submission that he would have never been able to get to without God's active leadership in his life.

As powerful and glorious as His rod is, I'm so grateful that Psalm 23 doesn't end with the rod. The Shepherd's use of the rod in our lives is so that we may become "partakers of His holiness." God has great and glorious plans for His children, and that's why He goes through the process of preparing us for our future; if He didn't, our future would crush us. It's when we've died with Him and been raised with Him, that we can walk into our destiny and not be crushed by it.

> You prepare a table before me in the presence of my enemies; You anoint my head with oil; my cup runs over. Surely goodness and mercy shall follow me all the days of my life; and I will dwell in the house of the LORD forever. (Ps. 23:5–6)

This scene is so vivid. God takes those who have come out of the valley of the shadow of death, and He sets them at a table in the presence of all their enemies: their internal enemies, their own hearts that condemned them and brought about hopelessness and despair; their invisible enemies, those accusers that tormented them, those devils that sought to kill, steal, and destroy them; and in some cases, their external enemies, those who sought their harm and rejoiced in their demise. The main point is that what God is about to do is public. He's making it dramatic for everyone to see.

God sits them down, takes a container of oil, opens it, and begins to pour it out on those who have endured. The anointing oil runs over their heads and down their bodies, filling them and overflowing every container.

I believe in days of public commissioning and anointing. I believe there are seasons in this life when God publicly vindicates and rewards those who stay the course and follow the Lamb through the valley. God continually takes His messengers through seasons of great trial into seasons of great blessing and commissioning. Whether it be Joseph in Egypt, or David, or John the Baptist, or the disciples on the Day of Pentecost, we continually see days of public vindication of a life of wisdom and humility.

> [John the Baptist] was in the deserts till the day of his manifestation to Israel. (Luke 1:80)

I also believe those who endure this life with all of its valleys, trials, and tribulations will receive great reward from the Lord Himself when they see Him.

> Blessed is the man who endures temptation; for when he has been approved, he will receive the crown of life which the Lord has promised to those who love Him. (James 1:12)

In the same way Jacob wrestled with "a Man" all night, received the blessing, and the rest of his life carried the mark of that night, so I believe that those who endure these seasons come out on the other side of it with a forever limp, but with a forever blessing (Gen. 32:24–32). What is the first tangible evidence of the oil being poured over the head in Psalm 23? — goodness and mercy following you all the days of your life. When a divine magnet is placed on your life attracting goodness and mercy, they will hunt you down, track you down, and find you **all the days of your life**.

What I love about this psalm is that David declares, "I will dwell in the house of the Lord forever." It's as if the greatest longing and desire of his life is that he would be placed in the house of the Lord forever. The greatest reward that a person could receive is proximity to God forever. As we looked at earlier in Revelation 7, one of the first rewards that the martyrs receive is to serve in the temple day and night, and to have God dwell among them.

Psalm 23 ends with the hope of dwelling in the house of the Lord forever. Our Shepherd's leadership is unto us living in the immediate presence of God for all eternity. This is the greatest longing of my heart, and I choose to say *yes* to whatever He has to do to get me to His house forever. No matter how dark that valley gets, just cling to Him because He is bringing you to His house.

Several months after God met me in Psalm 23, the Lord kept His promise to "make me lie down." Through a series of events, the

Lord made it clear that we as a family needed a sabbatical to receive ministry, healing, rest, and restoration. I desperately needed it, yet I didn't know how to make it happen. He made the arrangements. The first month away was just Dana and me, while God ministered to us individually and to our marriage. I honestly needed rest. I had plowed through for three years, doing my best to keep the family going, while at the same time traveling tons because doors were opening, God was moving, and I was needing to pay the bills. That first month was filled with a lot of sleeping, reading, receiving ministry, and exercising. I felt life coming back into me and was beginning to feel again, think again, and dream again.

It was during this time that Dana and I found each other again. We fell back in love and reconnected to each other and to our calling to see worship and prayer fill the earth. We were undone by the Hebrews 12 "author and perfecter of our faith" who was writing an amazing story with our family.

Soon after our kids joined us, and we saw the same healing and restoration take place in our family. It was a time we will never forget. One of the highlights of the summer was my thirteen-year-old daughter Mya's baptism. Toward the end of the summer, she began to desire to be baptized with water. It so happened that around that time Allen was coming up to see us, and we decided it would be a great time to do it.

Her baptism was absolutely amazing! It was filled with such a strong presence of the Holy Spirit and prophetic release, and it seemed God opened the heavens and shouted His pleasure over her. Two days later, our family was having a prayer meeting together and while Mya was leading, Dana went into travail; Mya was filled with the Spirit and began to sing in tongues as she led

10
Shepherds According to His Heart

I BELIEVE GOD IS EMPHASIZING THE revelation of Jesus as Shepherd because He is raising up shepherds in the earth in these days who can feed people with the knowledge of God's nature and heart, to stabilize others in their darkest nights. He must first shepherd them through their darkest nights to prepare them to shepherd the church during her coming days of glory and crisis.

I believe that Jesus' heart as a shepherd is being stirred as He scans the landscape of His beloved people Israel, the church, and the lost.

> Then Jesus went about all the cities and villages, teaching in their synagogues, preaching the gospel of the kingdom, and healing every sickness and every disease among the people. But **when He saw** the multitudes, **He was moved** with compassion for them, because they were weary and scattered, **like sheep having no shepherd**. Then He said to His disciples, "The harvest truly is plentiful, but the laborers are few. Therefore pray the Lord of the harvest to send out laborers into His harvest." (Matt. 9:35–38)

Here in Matthew 9, Jesus is in the middle of a revival, teaching, preaching, and healing. The crowds are growing, becoming multitudes, and we are given a holy glimpse into the soul of Jesus Christ. "**When He saw . . . He was moved**." These eyes of compassion are being restored to the church in our time. I want the eyes that see the multitudes not as numbers, tithers, or givers, but as weary and scattered sheep.

Jesus was deeply moved with compassion, and this is the heart of our Shepherd. He sees the weary, scattered, broken, and distressed, and He feels deep compassion. Jesus compares these ones to sheep having no shepherd. His deep compassion is born out of the many needs and the lack of qualified, prepared shepherds who know how to attend to the needs of the sheep.

He then looks at His disciples and causes them, as well as us, to grieve over the fact that the harvest is ready, but there are few shepherd-laborers. He calls us to take our pain and throw it into the furnace of prayer so the Lord of the harvest, the Shepherd of the sheep, would send forth shepherd-laborers into His harvest.

I believe that Psalm 23 will become more and more of an important chapter as we move closer to the generation of the Lord's return. God is bringing His people into His heart of compassion and calling them to the place of prayer unto being sent out. Soon in their journey, they will find out that when they jump into the furnace of prayer and fasting, God will begin to form them into the shepherds that resemble His Son. This includes deep affirmation as beloved sons and daughters as well as journeys through the valley of the shadow of death unto tables of commissioning. If we follow the Lamb wherever He goes, it will include the cross.

These ones will cling to Him as their only source and their only life, trusting Him as He guides them through the darkest of nights, brings them out on the other side, and anoints them in the presence of their enemies.

A great prophecy was given by Jeremiah to his generation, yet this prophecy includes something God will do in the last days, in both Israel and the nations:

> "I will give you shepherds according to My heart, who will feed you with knowledge and understanding." (Jer. 3:15)

Jeremiah peers into the future and sees a day coming when God will raise up leaders who have been fashioned according to His heart. They have followed the Shepherd/Lamb through the valley of the shadow of death and have come out on the other side; they can feed a generation with the knowledge of God. God took Moses through failure and loss of all identity before He could use him. He took him through a forty-year season of tending his father-in-law's flock in the seminary of the mundane as preparation for leading God's flock out of Egypt. He raised up a shepherd in David, who was trained through experiencing jealousy and betrayal. His father-in-law, the king, hunted him and sought to kill him because of God's call on his life. God used this to make David a shepherd for his generation. This kind of shepherd does not come cheaply, but is created through a process of God knitting their hearts to the heart of the Great Shepherd Himself, Jesus.

"**I will give**" is God's great gift to the earth of prepared messengers who can actually stabilize hearts during the great and terrible day of the Lord (spoken of in Acts 2:20). God has overseen the preparation of these messengers and has readied them for this hour. In Revelation 1, we see that Jesus holds seven stars in His hand. These stars, called "messengers," include the leaders and apostolic messengers for each of the seven churches. This shows His care, protection, preservation, and active engagement in their maturation as messengers. If you feel like you're not going to make it, just know He's holding you, friend.

"**Shepherds**" are not just messengers, but those who resemble the shepherd Jesus describes in John 10 — those who gather, strengthen, heal, restore, and go into the middle of the warfare instead of running off like hirelings when the thief is coming to steal, kill, and destroy. It's very significant that we see the Shepherd show up in John 10 in the context of a roaming, ravenous thief who is stealing, killing, and destroying weary, isolated, harassed sheep. Shepherds are those who fight for and defend, who run off every scheme of the evil one. These shepherds are leaders whose internal motivations are compassion and deep connection and burden over the welfare of the people.

"**According to My heart**" refers to the fact that God has prepared these shepherds in a specific seminary: the seminary of baptism into His heart. These shepherds have been joined to His heart and given insight into His emotions, His thoughts, and His purposes in such a profound way that they will be able to manifest His heart and intentions to a generation and bring restoration, healing, and leadership in the days of glory and shaking.

> "Let not the wise man glory in his wisdom, let not the mighty man glory in his might, nor let the rich man glory in his riches; but let him who glories glory in this, that he understands and knows Me, that I am the LORD, exercising lovingkindness, judgment, and righteousness in the earth. For in these I delight." (Jer. 9:23–24)

Understanding God has to be one of the rarest realities among humans, and yet God is going to raise up shepherds who understand Him, who get Him, and who manifest His nature to a generation. This is the dream of God — ones who do it like Him because they understand Him.

The anointing to understand God, to manifest and articulate His nature, is the baptism of fire into His heart — His broken, compassionate, zealous heart. When He begins to form your heart according to His heart, there is a divine disruption. When He gives a generation His eyes to see the weary, broken, and harassed, it's going to rearrange everything.

"**Who will feed you with knowledge and understanding**" means these shepherds will feed the earth with the revelation of God Himself. They will feed a generation with the Father, the Son, and the Spirit, with His heart, personality, nature, ability, and purposes and plans. The revelation of God alone is what stabilizes hearts. This will drive out fear, anxiety, torment, accusation, offense, and a multitude of other arrows from the evil one.

These shepherds will preach, teach, lead and play songs, and write books, lyrics, screenplays, documentaries, and films that feed a generation on God Himself. These shepherds will teach us how to eat by connecting them to the Word and the Spirit. Right now, all over the earth, God is raising up these shepherds according to His heart. They will come forth to stabilize the most fearful of hearts with the revelation of the beautiful and compassionate God.

Peter: A Shepherd According to His Heart

I began to search the Word, asking God, "Show me a shepherd You raised up and how You did it." David, at first, was the obvious answer to this. The one who began as a shepherd, who God took on the journey from fame and glory, to being hunted as a fugitive, to loss and recovery, to receiving kingship over Israel, is a perfect picture of how God raises up shepherds; yet it wasn't David who God led me to. **It was Peter.**

Peter's journey began at His feet in humiliation. After a long night of catching no fish, Jesus told him to throw the net on the other side of the boat. Begrudgingly, Peter did what He said and caught so many fish that the boat began to sink under their weight. From that moment, Peter, as well as the others, forsook everything and followed Him.

It was obvious from the beginning that he was a clear, bold leader. The initiative he took, the questions he asked, the ambition he possessed, and the dedication he exemplified were true marks of a natural-born leader. He was brought into the inner circle of fellowship and became one of the three who were given such an up-close-and-personal view of the life of Jesus. The things he saw, the words he heard, the miracles he witnessed, and the lessons he learned in that three-and-a-half year period are unspeakable. He was there on the mountain when Jesus began to pray and His face was altered, His clothes started to shine, Moses and Elijah showed up, and the Father spoke out of the cloud.

Peter is arguably the most favored person in history to have seen what he saw, heard what he heard, and lived what he lived with God in the flesh. In Matthew 16 it becomes clear that Peter will be one of the foundational pillars of the early church, and yet we see a faulty paradigm of authority and power that Jesus would have to correct in him before he could walk into the fullness of his destiny.

> When Jesus came into the region of Caesarea Philippi, He asked His disciples, saying, "Who do men say that I, the Son of Man,

> am?" So they said, "Some say John the Baptist, some Elijah, and others Jeremiah or one of the prophets." He said to them, "But who do you say that I am?" (vv. 13–15)

Before we move forward, we must at least pause to consider the magnitude of this question. If there was one thing that permeated Jewish culture, it was anticipation of the Jewish Messiah, the Deliverer who would come and deliver Israel from all her oppressors and establish her as chief among the nations. This was the longing of every sincere Jew, and the answer to this question Jesus posed carried the weight of thousands of years of anticipation of Israel's deliverance and thereby the nations of the earth.

"Simon Peter answered and said, 'You are the Christ, the Son of the living God'" (Matt. 16:16). These words are arguably the greatest ever uttered from human lips. To look at this common Man who didn't carry anything unique externally, and to discern and see Him as the Christ, the Anointed Messiah, the Son of David who was prophesied to come, is a supernatural work; and Peter, of all people, was given the high honor of receiving it and declaring it.

> Jesus answered and said to him, "Blessed are you, Simon Bar-Jonah, for flesh and blood has not revealed this to you, but My Father who is in heaven. And I also say to you that you are Peter, and on this rock I will build My church, and the gates of Hades shall not prevail against it. And I will give you the keys of the kingdom of heaven, and whatever you bind on earth will be bound in heaven, and whatever you loose on earth will be loosed in heaven." (Matt. 16:17–19)

Again, a *man* is receiving this blessing from Jesus Christ in the flesh. Peter was used by the Father to receive the revelation and declare the identity of Jesus as Messiah. Jesus then blessed him by declaring that He would build His church upon this revelation and that authority would be given Peter in heaven and earth. I honestly can't think of a greater honor being given to a man than being the recipient and declarer of the revelation that Jesus was Messiah. I imagine Peter was buzzing after this. It was a clearly distinguishing moment that separated him from everyone else. He was definitely in a high place of confidence coming off this encounter.

It's right here we see that though Peter was right concerning the identity of Jesus as Messiah, he had a faulty paradigm of the methodology by which the Messiah would fulfill the first phase of His deliverance of Israel. The next verses in Matthew 16 expose this faulty paradigm, which would serve as a crack in the dam that would play out over the next several months and culminate in Peter's denial of Jesus.

> From that time Jesus began to show to His disciples that He must go to Jerusalem, and suffer many things from the elders and chief priests and scribes, and be killed, and be raised the third day. Then Peter took Him aside and began to rebuke Him, saying, "Far be it from You, Lord; this shall not happen to You!" But He turned and said to Peter, "Get behind Me, Satan! You are an offense to Me, for you are not mindful of the things of God, but the things of men." (Matt. 16:21–23)

This is where Jesus throws a wrench in everything. He is going to turn all of the disciples' ideas of the Messiah on their heads by stating clearly that He was going to Jerusalem to suffer, die, and be raised again. If there was anything offensive to a Jewish mindset of Messiah, it was this statement. Messiahs don't suffer; they bring suffering to those who oppose God's will. They don't die; they do the killing. They don't surrender; they rule with a rod of iron.

It is with this mindset that **Peter takes Jesus to the side and begins to rebuke Him, saying, *Jesus, this will never happen to***

you. Before we get into this encounter between Jesus and Peter, I want to highlight the fact that a person can go from the heights of revelation to the depths of humiliation within a matter of minutes. There have been many days when I've left the prayer room feeling as if I was floating in the Holy Spirit, completely undone by God and the spirit of revelation, just to come home and, within minutes, say or do something that offends or disrespects a family member; I end up going straight into the flesh.

Peter, riding high off of the revelation just given to him and the public confirmation from Jesus, hears Him now talking about going to Jerusalem to suffer, die, and be raised again, and boldly steps in to correct Jesus. Peter is sincere, wanting to make it clear that this will never happen to Jesus as long as Peter is with Him. But Jesus sees this as something other than a sincere disciple wanting to show his loyalty; He sees it as Satan speaking through an unrenewed mind.

> But He turned and said to Peter, "Get behind Me, Satan! You are an offense to Me, for you are not mindful of the things of God, **but the things of men**." (Matt. 16:23)

The biggest strongholds that God has to confront and deal with in the preparation of His shepherds are the strongholds of success, greatness, impact, and strength *as defined by men.* It was this stronghold that ultimately led to Peter's denial, and Jesus showed no false mercy or grace in calling it what it is: an offense to Him. As Art Katz wrote in the introduction to his book *Apostolic Foundations*: "There is nothing more opposed to the purposes of God than the well-meaning intentions men perpetrate in their own human and religious zeal."

Jesus is confronting Peter's core issue — an unrenewed mindset concerning suffering, weakness, and loss. I'm convinced this same stronghold will cause many believers to fall away from the faith in the last days, becoming offended because the "god" they believed in would never allow suffering, loss, and difficulty.

Though this rebuke undoubtedly left an impact on Peter, it still was not enough to change him. It would take a more extreme collision for its truth to break in upon him. Fast forward to the last supper Jesus had with His disciples. Following His washing of the disciples' feet and Judas leaving to enact His betrayal, Jesus looked at the remaining disciples and said:

> "Little children, I shall be with you a little while longer. You will seek Me; and as I said to the Jews, '**Where I am going, you cannot come**,' so now I say to you." (John 13:33)

Jesus follows this (vv. 34–35) by highlighting the new commandment of loving one another and explaining that the world would know they were His through their love. Peter didn't even hear the new commandment, because he went back to Jesus' earlier statement and said, "'Lord, where are You going?'" (v. 36)

> Jesus answered him, "Where I am going you cannot follow Me **now**, but you shall follow Me **afterward**." Peter said to Him, "Lord, why can I not follow You now? I will lay down my life for Your sake." Jesus answered him, "Will you lay down your life for My sake? Most assuredly, I say to you, the rooster shall not crow till you have denied Me three times. Let not your heart be troubled; you believe in God, believe also in Me. In My Father's house are many mansions; if it were not so, I would have told you. I go to prepare a place for you. And if I go and prepare a place for you, I will come again and receive you to Myself; that where I am, there you may be also." (John 13:36–14:3)

Jesus knew that Peter wasn't listening to His new commandment, because as soon as Peter asked, "Where are You going?" Jesus answered quickly that he couldn't follow Him now, but would afterward. This is a key statement — Jesus was letting Peter know that something had to happen inside him before he could follow Jesus into the next season. What was the difference between Peter following Jesus now versus afterward? Could it be watching Jesus hanging on a cross, stripped naked; dying as a common criminal; and then being raised to life?

Peter truly wanted to be with Jesus, and it pained him to think of Jesus going somewhere he couldn't go. He thought that the only way he could keep up with Jesus was to show his unique devotion and sacrifice for the Lord. He remembered the events of Matthew 16, when Jesus told him that unless he took his cross and followed, he couldn't be Jesus' disciple. So Peter shot for the moon, stating to Jesus in front of the rest of the disciples that he would lay down his life.

Jesus looked him squarely in the eyes and said, *Will you really? By this time tomorrow morning, when the rooster crows, you will have denied Me three times.* Jesus continued on by saying, in essence, *When the revelation that you are not as dedicated as you think you are comes crashing in upon your life, don't give up. At that moment, believe in Me and my ability to bring you into the deepest longing of your heart: Abba's house, Abba's heart.*

Can you imagine the blow to the gut this was for Peter, as well as all the disciples? One of the gospels states that all the disciples began to vehemently oppose this statement; it was so offensive to these dedicated, loyal men. Yet all their ideas were about to come crashing down.

Later on the same evening, Jesus brought Peter, James, and John into the garden of Gethsemane, where the intensity of the hour began to bear down upon Jesus in increasing measure. He wanted these disciples to be with Him, to stay awake with Him, and to pray with Him, so that they would be able to navigate the coming dark night.

The last time that Jesus came back to awaken them was the moment that Judas and the soldiers entered the garden to bring about the great betrayal. Peter, quickly coming out of his sleep, arose to his feet, took a sword, and was going to prove once and for all his dedication and devotion to Jesus by going to death for Him. He swung with all of his might, ready to kill anyone who would seek to harm Jesus. Peter struck the High Priest's servant on the right ear, cutting it off. It's almost as if Peter looked up at Jesus and said, "Let's do this! I got your back! You are the Messiah. I'm with you. Let's start this thing now!"

Peter, waiting for Jesus' approval, hears the exact opposite as Jesus tells him to put the sword away.

> "Put your sword into the sheath. Shall I not drink the cup which My Father has given Me?" (John 18:11)

This was the final blow; it broke him. Every thought that he had ever had concerning the Messiah came crumbling down into a heap at that moment. Every dream that he ever had of ruling with Jesus collapsed in one second. The Messiah who would rule over Israel and the nations giving Himself to those guards, surrendering instead of fighting, was too much for Peter to handle.

Disillusioned Peter, watching as guards took Jesus away and, shaken to the core, began to follow at a distance with John to see what was going to happen to Jesus. Have you ever hit the wall that hard before? Have you ever come to a place where everything that you thought about God and yourself came crashing down? I'm convinced that this is part of God's seminary for His shepherds: the collapse of all of our secret fantasies of greatness and grandeur and ease.

As Jesus was brought before the Sanhedrin, Peter stumbled into the adjoining courtyard, completely undone. Everything that he had dreamed about concerning his future was destroyed in a moment, and everything he thought he knew about Jesus and himself was destroyed. He literally "didn't know Him" anymore (Luke 22:57). It's just like Satan to step into these moments to take advantage of us in our most vulnerable and shaken season and to try to disqualify us for the next season. Earlier in the evening, Jesus had told Peter,

> "Simon, Simon! **Satan has asked for you, that he may sift you as wheat. But I have prayed for you**, that your faith should not fail; and when you have returned to Me, strengthen your brethren." (Luke 22:31–32)

Jesus spoke this phrase to Peter, telling him that Satan came and asked if he could take Peter out. Jesus basically told him, *Try your best, but on one condition: I get to pray for him.* Friend, I want you to know that there are "opportune seasons" that come around when the enemy will seek to take you out in one of your most vulnerable places. As he seeks to disqualify you and destroy your life, know this: you have an intercessor at the right hand of the Father praying you through it. Jesus told Peter that he would stumble and he would go away, but that he would return from it, and his testimony would be strength to many.

It was in this crisis moment that Satan set in motion his scheme to disqualify the "Rock" on which the church would be built. Over the next several hours, we see three different people, at three different times through the night, ask Peter the same question, "Aren't you one of the disciples of Jesus?" With each answer, Peter denied knowing Jesus, very adamantly separating himself from anything to do with Him.

I've heard people in the past say, "How in the world could Peter have done this?" I understand what they are saying, but I'm also deeply aware of what happens in our minds and hearts when something that was so rock solid in our ideas concerning God and ourselves and our future is broken in a moment, and for a season we don't know Him like we thought we knew Him. Everything that we built our life upon appears to us as a farce, and we think if this wasn't solid, then maybe none of it is. I literally believe that when Jesus surrendered to those soldiers, Peter's theology was shaken to the core. When he said he didn't know Him, he meant it!

> But Peter said, "Man, I do not know what you are saying!" Immediately, while he was still speaking, the rooster crowed. And the Lord turned and looked at Peter. Then Peter remembered the word of the Lord, how He had said to him, "Before the rooster crows, you will deny Me three times." So Peter went out and wept bitterly. (Luke 22:60–62)

The numbness that Peter had been living in for the past few hours came to a crashing end as the rooster crowed. All of a sudden, the realization of what he had done hit him like a ton of bricks, and to make matters worse, Luke includes the fact that the "the Lord turned and looked at Peter." The Lord, who had endured a night of interrogation, beating, and ridicule looked at him, and the words of his denials came in like a wrecking ball.

"**Peter went out and wept bitterly**." I don't think words can do adequate justice to what Peter felt in this moment. I'm convinced with all my heart that it was Jesus' prayers for him that kept him from hanging himself like Judas as this realization hit him.

The next hours leading up to Jesus' crucifixion, and the days following, are only known to God as Peter fought tooth and nail against the tormenters and accusers. We know he wasn't there at the cross. Where was he? How did he keep from completely losing it? Jesus' prayers. What kept him from suicide? Jesus' prayers. I cannot even imagine the depths of pain that struck his heart during those days, but I do know what it feels like to have your world shaken to its core and to be tormented day and night by the fear that the ones you love won't make it.

I remember when my wife and I were in our early years of marriage, and she was pregnant with our first daughter. We decided to do our last getaway trip before our daughter came. We literally had no money, and it was only because of a gift from my grandmother that we were able to go. On this trip, we were hanging out in a Christian bookstore when we saw a painting and immediately fell in love with it. It was by Eugène Burnand of John and Peter running to the tomb on resurrection day. It was so detailed and impactful that we took all of the money we had left ($250) and bought the painting; we have it to this day. The artist painted it with such detail and insight into Peter and John and what they were feeling, their anticipation and their fear.

We don't know exactly where Peter was for those three days after the crucifixion, but we know he "made it," because Mary Magdalene came first to both Peter and John after discovering that Jesus' body was missing. Peter immediately started running toward the tomb. I love this. He undoubtedly had tons of fears, anxieties, and pain over what just happened, but somehow in the midst of it all, he knew to run toward God instead of from Him. That's the way I want to be.

Over the next several days, the resurrected Lord appeared to the disciples many times, and though we don't see any direct encounters between Peter and Jesus, we know that they saw each other, embraced one another, and had moments together. But as far as we know, the elephant in the room, Peter's denial, was never addressed. I think a point we can take from this is that before Jesus would address it, He wanted to wash Peter for a season in His love and affection for him and let that restore Peter's confidence.

After a little over a week of encounters with Jesus, it was time to address Peter's deepest pain and his calling. We find the story revealed in John 21, where we see that Peter and seven others decided to "go fishing." I have no doubts in my mind that Peter was seriously entertaining Plan B for his life. Someone who had grown up a fisherman, had been around it his whole life, and who had to be thinking after the denials that any future in ministry was over, went fishing as an escape from the pain of his failure, and also as a reentry into the only thing that he had ever done: fish.

To add insult to injury, Peter found that even his Plan B was a failure; once again, he fished all night to catch absolutely nothing. He was brought to the end of his rope, in complete despair and hopelessness, and yet the dawn was beginning to come forth and the silence of that night was shattered by a simple phrase: "**Children, have you any food?**" (John 21:5). The question is to bring them and us to the painful revelation that outside of Him, we can do nothing. When they confessed that they didn't have any, they heard a command that brought them (especially Peter) back to the first time they met Jesus: "Cast the net on the right side of the boat, and you will find some" (v. 6). Once again, it was a huge catch.

John, looking at Peter, declared, "**It is the Lord**!" (v. 7). As soon as Peter heard it was Him, he jumped into the water and began to swim to Jesus. What strikes me here is that the first time Peter met Jesus an almost identical scenario transpired where they had caught nothing, Jesus told them to cast the net to the other side, and they caught a huge amount. The first time this happened, Peter fell down at Jesus' feet and told Him to depart from him because he was a sinful man; yet this time, when the revelation of who Jesus was struck him, Peter swam *to* Him. Though not directly stated, it seems to me that Peter had come to a powerful revelation about running *to* Jesus in his weakness versus running *from* Him in his weakness.

Before we go into the climatic last scene of Peter's failure and encounter with Jesus, I want to highlight again what happens for those who walk through and endure the valley of the shadow of death: God prepares a table for them, sits them down, and in the presence of their enemies He anoints their heads with oil, commissioning them, healing them, and restoring them. What we are about to witness in Peter's experience is the same process described in Psalm 23 — how God raises up shepherds according to His heart. Peter is about to discover what God does for those who endure the valley of the shadow of death.

> Then, as soon as they had come to land, they saw a fire of coals there, and fish laid on it, and bread. Jesus said to them, "Bring some of the fish which you have just caught." . . . Jesus said to them, "Come and eat breakfast." (John 21:9–10, 12)

The breakfast table has been set and the resurrected Son is about to serve Peter (as well as the other disciples) a meal. He sits Peter down, fixes a meal for him, and honors him at the table.

He waits until breakfast is over before He addresses the elephant in the room: Peter's huge claims of love and devotion, his miserable failure, and the question of whether he is going to be useful in this next season of ministry. We must consider here what God does to prepare leaders when He is birthing a movement. He must utterly destroy their self-reliance and bring them to the end of themselves before He can use them. He wants leaders who are broken, dependent on Him and each other, and who all know each other's stories. This is what is about to happen around the breakfast table.

> So when they had eaten breakfast, Jesus said to Simon Peter, "Simon, son of Jonah, do you love Me more than these?" He said to Him, "Yes, Lord; You know that I love You." He said to him, "**Feed My lambs**." He said to him again a second time, "Simon, son of Jonah, do you love Me?" He said to Him, "Yes, Lord; You know that I love You." He said to him, "**Tend My sheep**." He said to him the third time, "Simon, son of Jonah, do you love Me?" Peter was grieved because He said to him the third time, "Do you love Me?" And he said to Him, "Lord, You know all things; You know that I love You." Jesus said to him, "**Feed My sheep**." (John 21:15–17)

After they had eaten breakfast, Jesus asks the same question three times regarding Peter's love and devotion. "**Do you love Me?**" This question undoubtedly brought back to Peter's mind the very phrases that had come out of his mouth just a little over a week earlier as he boldly declared that though others would falter, he would go all the way to death for Jesus. These questions were exposing and humbling, yet at the same time were validating and affirming what was real on the inside of Peter.

The first two times Jesus asked Peter if he loved Him, He used the word *agape* for love. This agape love is the highest form of love and expresses the love that God has for us — a love that is completely free and unmerited. It's the self-sacrificing love that Jesus expressed at the cross. Jesus is asking, *Do you love Me with the intense and selfless love that you thought you did?* Peter's answer is striking as he responds with, "Yes, Lord; You know that I love You," but his word for love is *phileo* which means affectionate, brotherly love. Peter is responding to Jesus' question with, "I don't love you with the same intensity or depth that I thought I loved you; but I do love you, and it's real."

This is a massive moment in church history. The "Rock" Simon Peter, one of the primary pillars of the early church, publicly declared his weak, yet real love to God in the presence of his enemies. In this case, his enemies were the tormenting and accusing voices that constantly bombarded him with thoughts and emotions of disqualification. Each time Peter declared his love for Jesus, each arrow of each denial was ripped out of his heart, thereby breaking the power of the accuser and tormenters. Why did Jesus ask Peter this question? **Because Peter needed to hear himself openly declare his weak, yet real love for Jesus.** This broke the power of the evil one and caused the "oil" of healing to come and the "oil" of commissioning to be released in his life.

Beloved, I believe God is taking His shepherds through similar stories, where at the moment of our complete brokenness and inability to do anything, He brings us to the table and calls forth a declaration of our love for Him. It's at this table that He takes His oil and pours it over our lives, and then He heals, restores, and commissions us for the next season.

What is Jesus going to do with Peter's (as well as our) public realization of our sincere, yet weak love? Is He going to rebuke us? Correct us? Or is He going to look at us and say, *Yeah, I know . . . and you know what? That'll work for Me. You in touch with reality is what will release the oil of commissioning over your life to "Feed My lambs." I have need of you Peter, and out of your own brokenness, you are going to feed My lambs. I'm entrusting you with My people, My church.* Here is where we see the Great Shepherd, Jesus, bringing forth His "shepherds according to My heart" to feed His lambs. The oil pours over Peter, healing, restoring, and empowering him for the next season.

The third time Jesus asked Peter if he loved Him, He didn't use *agape*; He used *phileo*. So Jesus is asking Peter, *Do you love Me like a brother, with affection?* Peter answered, "Yes, Lord, that's the way I love You." It was in this third time that both Peter and Jesus were in agreement over the nature of Peter's love, and once again, Jesus commissioned him, calling him to, "**Feed My sheep**."

Before we move on from these three questions, I want you to know that God wants to bring all of His shepherds to the table and have us confront our greatest fears, failures, and losses by looking Him in the eyes and declaring our love for Him. As I stated earlier, our family took a four-month sabbatical in 2016. If there was one thing that I can state clearly that God did in me during those months, it was this. In areas where I felt that I failed Him, my family, and myself, God sat me down at His table and spoke again and again His pleasure over me. As I believed these things and agreed with them, I felt His healing and power touching me.

When I stated, "You know I love you," I could feel a thousand lies destroyed and a new commissioning coming on my family and me. I spent the majority of those months contemplating this encounter between Peter and Jesus, and I was massively strengthened and encouraged as I saw Jesus' brilliant leadership and heart toward His shepherds.

> "Most assuredly, I say to you, when you were younger, you girded yourself and walked where you wished; but when you are old, you will stretch out your hands, and another will gird you and carry you where you do not wish." This He spoke, signifying by what death he would glorify God. And when He had spoken this, He said to him, "Follow Me." (John 21:18–19)

After Jesus addressed Peter's deepest pain and failure and restored him, He told him that things were changing from that moment on. In essence, He tells him that, *Up until this moment, you've done things out of your strength, girding yourself, walking where you wished, and doing it your way; but from this moment on, you will live out of your weakness and dependence on God, not your strength and independence.* Jesus is ultimately speaking of Peter's death, but it includes this paradigm shift into a life of dependence on God. After Jesus established this, He gave Peter his greatest longing: the desire to follow Jesus. Do you remember earlier in John 13 when Jesus told him that he couldn't follow Him now, but would follow Him afterward? Jesus is now telling Peter, *Now is the afterward. You are ready to follow Me and to lead like I lead, because you've walked through the valley of the shadow of death and come out on the other side.*

Many years later, when Peter's time came for him to die, history tells us that instead of being crucified like Jesus, Peter asked them to crucify him upside down, because he was unworthy to die like His Lord. Jesus gave him his greatest prayer: he was able to lay down his life for Jesus.

> Then Peter, turning around, saw the disciple whom Jesus loved following . . . Peter, seeing him, said to Jesus, "But Lord, what about this man?" Jesus said to him, "If I will that he remain till I come, what is that to you? You follow Me." (John 21:20–22)

Apparently, after breakfast and during the questions, Jesus and Peter went on a walk, because after Jesus spoke with him, Peter turned around and saw John following them. Asked about John's fate, Jesus tells Peter, in essence, *Don't worry about his or anyone else's journey, but you do what I've called you to do: follow Me.*

Friends, don't get caught in comparison with anyone else's journey in God. God will raise up a thousand shepherds in a thousand different ways, and we cannot build one model out of it. We can't look to the left or to the right, but we must set our eyes on the Lamb, and follow Him wherever He goes. Let Him lead you through your valley, and let Him lead you to your mountain.

I can so identify with Peter's story and Jesus' journey of making him a shepherd. From day one of my salvation, I walked in great favor from the Lord, experiencing deep revelation of His heart and of His nature. I've had a very clear sense of leadership and calling on my life, yet like Peter, I had a faulty paradigm about weakness. Through these last five years, the Lord has slowly brought all of my best attempts to "save" our family to nothing. My constant need to fix everyone only made things worse and actually caused my girls' hearts to go further from me. My words, which have been used countless times to set many free, only put yokes and weights on my family's hearts, and the continual reminders of this only made me try harder to come up with the puzzle piece that would unlock their hearts and save the day. Just like Peter, I kept trying; and just like Peter, I kept failing. I refused to listen to the resounding siren going off in my life and in my family. God was basically saying, *Corey, I don't need you fix or save anyone. I need you to be with them, and weep with them, and just listen.* To me, this felt like He was saying to be passive, but it actually exposed my unbelief that God would get us out of this mess. The revelation of the Shepherd, in my weakest moment, allowed me to be shepherded by Him, so that I could, for the first time, say, "I don't have any answers and solutions. I just have a simple trust that He will lead us out of this." God must bring all of us to this point, so that He can manifest His power in us and through us.

This same Peter stepped out of the upper room fifty days later, into the very streets where he had denied Jesus, and boldly called the nations to repent and believe on the Lord Jesus Christ. He was entrusted with the first message of the church. Three thousand were cut to the heart and cried out to be saved. The book of Acts began. Who leads like Jesus? Who brings forth leaders like Jesus? There is no one.

Conclusion

TODAY, AS I WRITE THIS CONCLUSION, it's June 26, 2017. This is Nash's birthday, and he would be turning five years old. As I drove to the prayer room this morning, I told him "happy birthday" and how grateful to God I am that he was born. As I heard myself say that, I was flooded with emotions of great happiness over the memories that we did have with him during his short time on earth, and I also thought of all the painful memories since his death. As I think about my son, his life, his death, and the impact it's had on our family, I thank God. I thank God because for nine-and-a-half months, I experienced the joy of having and holding and kissing and playing with my son. I thank God because today I'm less confident in my own ability and leadership and more confident in His ability and leadership. I thank God because of the tenacity, courage, and resilience I've seen in my wife and daughters. I thank God because we are here, loving God and each other.

It's on days like today that I rest in the fact that my relationship with my son is not over, but that we will stand face to face again, and we will embrace. I don't know whether he will be a one year old or a thirty year old, but I do know that everything in me will explode with emotions of deep joy at that moment. (I'm really looking forward to that moment!)

I'm a different man than I was five years ago. My family is a different family, and we've been eternally changed. God is still in the process of putting us back together again, but He isn't putting us back together into what we were, but into something that we've never been before. We are a work in process, but I believe we will look back in thirty years on this season and see that, in spite of one of the most horrible of tragedies, God brought forth a glorious testimony of His goodness and faithfulness.

God has used these five psalms as specific revelations of His heart and purpose, and they have carried us through the darkest of nights. **Because of Psalm 132**, I know that I have one moment, called this life, to go "all out" in living a life of "one thing" and laboring to see His house raised up all over the earth. I believe that the choices I make in this life move God and release great eternal promises. I will go through any affliction to see God's fame established in the earth through worship and prayer in the nations.

Because of Psalm 1 and 2, I know God's Word is to be to me a place of delight, pleasure, fascination, and revelation. In the midst of a generation that is seeking to throw off God's Word and leadership, I'm called to come underneath the leadership of the Word of God. I want to be a tree in this generation that has deep roots and that prospers in every season. I want to be a man of prayer, who in the midst of my places of greatest warfare, will contend and see the greatest inheritance.

One of my greatest inheritances is to labor to see Nasharites arise all over the earth, who will pray in the greatest outpouring of the Holy Spirit ever. They are hidden intercessors who will lay hold of God to see historic revival released. They may never be known to men, but they will be famous in heaven. They will be rooted in their identity as sons, and they will confidently ask the Father for Jesus' inheritance in their nation, as well as all the nations.

Because of Psalm 91, I am fully confident that in Him there is protection from *every* assault of the evil one. Under His wings, I'm covered. Because of His angels, I'm carried. That which the enemy sought to kill me with actually strengthened me to tread upon the lion and the cobra. Psalm 91 told me that when I set my love upon God, He will deliver me, elevate me, answer my prayers, be with me, honor me, satisfy me with long life, and will show me His salvation.

Because of Psalm 18, I saw the "angry God," who makes my enemies, His enemies. When I cry out to him in my darkest hour, He will intervene with great zeal and fierce anger as He openly confronts those who seek to kill me. He exposes everything, laying it all bare, and he comes in like a Navy SEAL team delivering a POW, and delivers me because He delights in me. His deliverance of me makes me a deliverer and increases in me the strength to get through impossible situations, as I learn how to fight the enemy and set others free.

Because of Psalm 23, I met Jesus the Shepherd and was commissioned by Him to be a shepherd to my family and to this generation. At a time when I was beginning to break, Jesus showed up and asked if He could minister to and shepherd me. That simple question changed everything. He brought me to a place of quiet dependence and rest, a place of self-reflection, and I found Him with me in the valley of the shadow of death. I found my wife, my family, and myself again. He set a table before me and, in the presence of all the enemies who sought to destroy me, He poured oil over me and commissioned me to be a shepherd in His house.

These five psalms have been my best friends for five years. They gave language for my heart when I didn't have language. Jesus spoke them over me when I didn't have anything to say. They helped me get above the storms so that I could see another day. These psalms gave me hope and faith when I didn't have any. They provoked me, strengthened me, comforted me, and ministered deeply to me. I don't know where I would be without these five psalms.

And yet I know that our small story is but one of many that God is taking His people through in this hour. The Great Shepherd is raising up shepherds everywhere, in every sphere and in every nation of the earth. As Jesus is scanning the nations, seeing the weary, scattered, and harassed sheep, compassion is welling up within Him, and He is coming up with an answer. His answer to this crisis is to take His beloved ones through intense seasons that will release deep compassion within them, causing them in turn to release healing and deliverance to many.

In the same way we can trust our Shepherd to lead us through the valley because He's been there, so God will raise up men, women, marriages, and families others can trust because they've "been there," too. They will come into impossible situations and with understanding, clarity, compassion, and anointing, will help bring healing and deliverance and restoration. They will manifest the nature of God, and they will make the needy feed on God.

In an hour when marriages and families are being destroyed, God has an ace card up His sleeve — marriages and families that didn't quit and didn't throw it away. They chose to forgive, to love, and to fight for the promises of God. When they thought there was no chance of restoration, God broke in and turned their hearts.

I'm so filled with hope for our future as well as your future, and I believe that the greatest places of our warfare will truly become the greatest places of our inheritance.

Word from a Friend

When I read in the Psalms about the Lord taking our feet out of the miry clay, setting us on a rock, and putting a new song in our mouth, I think of Corey Russell.

I have known Corey for more than twenty years. It was his testimony of the Lord rescuing him out of a dark world of rebellion and drugs that captured our family's attention and love. His song is fiery and passionate about a good and merciful God whose ways are higher. Corey, since his salvation, has never settled for less than all that God has promised.

I have witnessed, once again, that same radical passion of clinging to God when Corey and his family faced the death of his only son, Nash. Having experienced the loss of three children of my own, I fully know and understand how few are willing and brave enough to trust God when their vision of His goodness is blurred by tears of anguish. I am convinced that such focused trust in the midst of what feels like a suffocating experience becomes a shield from the dark weapons of accusation and blame.

I love Corey like a son. He makes me laugh and he inspires me. He is unabashed and unashamed. He is worthy to be heard either through his writing or speaking. To observe his life, one cannot deny that the Lord is real, and His love is enough!

Judy Swift

Corey's long-time friends the Swifts ministered to the Russells in the days following Nash's death.